#postdildo

ALSO BY DANIELLE LaFRANCE

*Friendly + Fire**

*JUST LIKE I LIKE IT**

species branding

*Published by Talonbooks

#postdildo

poems

DANIELLE LAFRANCE

talonbooks

Talonbooks
9259 Shaughnessy Street, Vancouver, British Columbia, Canada V6P 6R4
talonbooks.com

Talonbooks is located on xʷməθkʷəy̓əm, Sḵwx̱wú7mesh, and səl̓ilwətaʔɬ Lands

First printing: 2022

Typeset in Avenir Next
Printed and bound in Canada on 100% post-consumer recycled paper

Cover design and cover illustrations by Ginger Sedlarova
Interior photographs by Danielle LaFrance
Typset by Typesmith

Talonbooks acknowledges the financial support of the Canada Council for
the Arts, the Government of Canada through the Canada Book Fund, and the
Province of British Columbia through the British Columbia Arts Council and
the Book Publishing Tax Credit.

Library and Archives Canada Cataloguing in Publication

Title: #Postdildo : poems / Danielle LaFrance.
Other titles: Post dildo
Names: LaFrance, Danielle, 1983- author.
Identifiers: Canadiana 20220257825 | ISBN 9781772014372 (softcover)
Classification: LCC PS8623.A368 P67 2022 | DDC C811/.6–dc23

This project is dedicated to past, present, and future carnal writings, positionings, and imagings - whether they cum or not.

And to a rare garbage person and an alien fur-friend, who both know it and feel it, or at least woof it and meow it.

You + I encounter a bright-red city garbage dumpster marked by a graffiti tag that reads, "post-dildo."

— It's a new turn: post-dildo.
You raise an eyebrow.

— Well, what does that mean?
— You + I must fashion new fantasies.
— Well, I'mma give it to ya.

—September 15, 2016

Cuntents

#intr●ducti●n

#postdildo

or

AFTER DELIGHTS

or

A DISCLAIMER

You might be wondering, "What the fuck is post-dildo?" Already the word "dildo" is suspect, its etymology uncertain. Perhaps from the beautiful Italian word "diletto," a masculine noun for pleasure, delight? From the Latin "dilectio," esteem, love? Dildos are delightful and loveable. I hope You agree with this.

I am going to keep it real with You. Not Lacanian real. I am going to offer a bit of an in for You, if only just the tip, to the mess, the muddled middle, the ambiguous grab bag of resisting and contradictory materials that make up post-dildo. post-dildo is so You + I might live differently and better, just maybe. In this grab bag, You will find a dildo, a red marker, a cock, and a sucker. These are tools that owe their existence to ideas put forward by other ideas, but when assembled and cut a hole through which to usher You + I into a world.

While midstep of a song and dance to get some money, I asked, "How shall You fuck without causing harm?" I wrote a proposal in the midst of #MeToo (a term coined by Tarana Burke to found a movement in 2006 and later used by mostly white celebrities in 2017), as a collective reckoning proliferated on screens, catalyzing charged call-outs and -ins, all demanding response, that would never, ever be satisfied. You + I, slimed by all kinds of differences, recalled visceral sexual experiences. Some experiences mapped onto others' experiences, bringing the past into the present, as trauma does. Four years later I believe this moment to have been one that concretized and validated the horror imposed upon bodies – more often trans, non-binary, feminized, Two-Spirit, and racialized ones – without consent, while also offering no real resolution, no real difference to how You + I live past critique, even past action. This reckoning drew lines in the quicksand; some friends are gone now and some friends continue to get whatever they want.

Meanwhile, in the background of relational ordeals, I encountered a graffiti tag on the side of a dumpster – a ubiquitous, tentacular slut of an idea, rife with violence: "post-dildo." That initial brush with garbage in 2016 offered an opening to think and write through the limitlessness and limitations of sexuality communication, and desire. post-dildo (d) evolved from graffiti tag to hashtag. #postdildo culminated in a series of curated images with the intent of capturing the discursive, viscous essence of this new cultural (sexual? political?) turn. What came before #postdildo if not internet porn, the confession booth, colonial capitalism, settler sexuality, patriarchy, and *feminism*, all providing a blueprint for how to be touched and fucked, inadequately.

Breakups incited upheavals and several tragedies spawned this anchor to hang my finite life from the tips of my uncut toenails, glossing a mode to relate and not relate through: the hydraulics of sex. Such a mode requires destruction, construction, endings, remixes, upheavals, swallowings – You know, the kind of repetition masquerading as difference that, on occasion, You + I gobble up as reassurance that You + I are eating from the same bowl of knowing what the actual fuck is going on between You + I. It's diletto! I see #postdildo acting as a screen – a filter? – for me, and perhaps You, to *be* in the contradiction(s) of feminism, of fantasy, of sexual violence, and of communicating about it, all in a way that will never satisfy. It feels impossible to exist outside of rape culture, and it seems even harder to divide sexual violence from some kind of pure sexual desire. Maybe just a few glorious bites of pleasure and a politics of desire could be mixed into the bag of suckers.

From its beginnings, #postdildo has housed a number of assemblages, one of which was a reading group that I held on stolen and occupied xʷməθkʷəy̓əm, Sḵwx̱wú7mesh, and səl̓ilwətaʔɬ Lands during the summer of 2018. Maybe You were there? Five sessions loosely guided participants towards responses that reflected upon the contradictory terrains of fantasy and violence and communication. This book, *#postdildo*, dredges up a lot, too much, pursuing unknowns across pages littered with non sequiturs. The reading group and its groundwork helped conjure up much of the book's fodder. My hope is that the book talks *with* You, although it might occasionally talk *at* You after a few gusanos de maguey. The book might be sorry in the morning and regret its apology by the evening.

You + I expanded and contracted, sometimes You + I got there, sometimes You + I hovered over it, and mostly You + I pulsed towards some kind of mutual grotesque critter, sincerely trying to carry all the shit in tandem. But what the fuck is the shit? If there is one thing that Lacanian psychoanalysis has taught me, it's the almost desperate way the social subject piecemeals what's left after a rupture, applying whatever resources are available, whatever logic or model, to get I's shit together. #postdildo holds our shit together. #postdildo shat it out down a leg every interview.

Meanwhile, the dildo became a relational tool to contend with so-called messy relationships – messy because of the hegemonic scripts You + I have inherited and continue to internalize. You + I speak and act accordingly. Same as You + I act out. In "The Dildo as a Transformative Political Tool: Feminist and Queer Perspectives,"[1] Arpita Das notably writes on the dildo as a means to support both sexual autonomy and alienation. What makes a dildo special is that it's a ready-made prosthetic, available, and detached from any supposed owner who may cause damage. As the saying goes: "Dildos don't kill people, people kill people." While I continue to yearn for relations that produce new use values for a decapitalized society (I'm keeping this one too, sweetie), the unconscious investment in ideology oiled by the logic of capitalism, patriarchy, colonialism, and white supremacy keeps me in a feedback loop; I'm in the contradiction, whether I want to be or not. This ideology ("You and your fucking ideology!") is culturally and socially constructed. It seeps through bodies, drips off speech acts and policies. It is pervasive and I don't know how to deal with it, so I turn to a graffiti tag on a dumpster as a conduit through which to combat this double bind.

Dildos are not the enemy, but they could be if You + I want them to be. #postdildo is in no way against dildos; in fact, it believes in the ubiquity and proliferation of them. I am greatly indebted to Paul B. Preciado's body-essays; he gargled and spat out new life into how I imagine dildos: as just another tool. The dildo is a split possibility, just as every organ becomes something else with a little imagination outside the old heterosexual regime. You + I are ensnared in the logic of these dreaded scripts You + I are ready to burn over and over again until You + I get it right. Preciado describes the dildo's logic as one that first terrifies, "It's death stalking the living penis," then possesses – "loss of sexual sovereignty in order to finally gain a plastic pleasure"[2] – and finally sublimates and surpasses all organs, returning to the body in order to multiply its pleasures. It is so good to be fucked by death. It is so good to be fucked without anything to show for it other than a persistent UTI. I wouldn't have it any other way. #postdildo presents a cacophony of living and resurrected octopus arms reaching out to love You + I with their three hearts, laying their eggs in our welcoming orifice as they die another day after birth. If a dildo turns prosthetics against organs for the transformative purpose of deterritorializing them, #postdildo is the shared cigarette smoked with a dildo after they tell You they'll never leave You.

What kind of new script am I after? What kind of new fantasy? What kind of sex am I looking for? A decapitalized world without "work-life balance" because there is only life and death, a world without policing desires and desiring police because there are no police, a world where non-procreative sexuality holds value because families are communal and chosen. #postdildo wants to play with those who are down to play. No pressure. In Preciado's world, everything is over and it's up to You + I to slurp up all the same old and shit it back out again. #postdildo fingers an open antagonism that peels beyond the violence adhered to sensual relations. There is some relief with this prodding, some utopic fantasy even where reinvented shit holds all the kernels (have You heard of the corn test?) from the past and now You + I get to see it for what it's worth.

#postdildo delves into more shit. With the intellectual help of Kay Higgins, I returned to how a history of resigning to cis male "genius" and its pursuit of mastery sets the conditions that govern the apex of so much of our production and value. This is further unpacked in "Maso and Miso in the Land of Men's Rights,"[3] where Élisabeth Lebovici and Giovanna Zapperi contend with one hundred notable French women who took issue with the #MeToo movement. White French cis women like Catherine Deneuve framed #MeToo as being an unfair counter to masculine nature and integrity; that French (white) cis men have a right to objectify and dominate, because otherwise they would be acting against their authentic mode of being. Basically You + I have to take it, just because history and tradition say so. This logic has You + I shaking our heads, not because of what actions are condoned but because of the expectation of authenticity precluding any other way to be, that the territory assumed is a given and it's the primary domain of cis men to act. The problem for You + I is how engagement with Catherine's position can find You + I uncomfortably taking on the position as a central antagonism, the position offered credence by the sheer act of discourse production. Should You + I ignore it, turn the other's cheek, or challenge, or …? You + I contend with this by reformulating the discourse over and over again ad nauseam, where You + I get stuck in the same circular argument, but the repetition is worth it, so You + I can get it just right enough to let it go.

I remember wanking (I used to fuck a pillow and a stuffed toy gorilla until there was a death in the family and I thought their ghost was watching me) to Catherine's famous tits brushing against Susan Sarandon's, but when I read her spew shit about French men having the right to disturb ("déranger" in French), my fingers went flaccid. *But* I got hard again rethinking about the hysteric (perhaps even my #MeToo-driven hysteric) as a counter to cis male genius and what the hysteric could look like now as a subject that breaks time, never picking up the pieces, never following through, wrapped in the shroud of their mess. Georges Didi-Huberman writes how "the hysteric defies the spectator's desire, consecrates and defies her mastery."[4] The hysteric elicits scrutiny from all those who subscribe to cis male genius, because they disturb the status quo of the moment by viscerally remembering other times and cultures that are outside the assumed structure of cis male genius. You + I are so much more, so much less, than these assumptions that have only cohered through time and practice.

#postdildo splooshes and splashes in the contradiction. Alenka Zupančič writes how "it's not about accepting the contradiction, but about *taking one's place in it*."[5] There is something here about the erotic charge of contradiction that excites as much as it depresses and gets You + I forever stuck flexing familiar antidotes to late capitalism: "Everything must go," writes comrade and poet Ted Rees.[6] Fixed positions are always rubbing up against other fixed positions. #postdildo wants to dislodge You + I from our fixities and become deluded feminists out to stop time.

#postdildo is not against pleasure; it might find pleasure in refusal. You + I want to propose a type of writing on sex where a tidal wave meets another tidal wave. In other words, You + I want to make each other squirt and dribble. You + I can still, of course, question and critique where our fantasies, our pleasures, derive from. In many cases a rape fantasy is the only way You + I can reach orgasm. In "Letter from a Trans Man to the Old Sexual Regime," Preciado calls for desires to be transformed, stating that we must learn how to desire sexual freedom. "Come to grips with your shadowy side," he writes, "and have fun with it."[7] I think of Nancy Friday's erotic retellings of women's rape fantasies, which You + I never talked about during the reading group session – funny, because so much of this work hinges on violence that I want to recuperate and reclaim through fantasy and play. You + I were perhaps too shy to go there. In the chapter "Room Number Three: Rape, or, 'Don't Just Stand There, Force Me!,'" Friday succinctly tells her reader that "the message isn't in the plot – the old hackneyed rape story – but in the emotions that story releases."[8] While my rape fantasy has nothing to do with some kind of wish fulfillment for actual rape and has everything to do with a calibre of release only achieved with the most trustworthy of You, it would be remiss of me not to trouble my shadowy side. The difference, of course, between kink and harm is consent. One is catharsis from trauma and the other is trauma.

There *really* is not that much to say about rape culture that has not already been said. #postdildo wants to allow for all the room in sexual fantasies, especially when applying criticism from a feminist Marxist lens, moving beyond the false consciousness where our fantasies are not our own, solely dictated by capitalist white-supremacist patriarchy. How much power and agency do You + I want to ascribe to these brutalizing scripts? What came first? My rape or my rape fantasy? And what are my politics around feminism now that there's a herd of TERFs having me now hate the word "radical" and a swarm of SWERFs having me hate the word "work"? This is not the feminism You + I were look-ing for. Second-wave feminism has my sexual fantasies placed on the chopping block in order to alter a world not yet known to You + I. As Amia Srinivasan so wonderfully states in *The Right to Sex*: "The ques-tion posted by radical self-love movements is not whether there is a right to sex (there isn't), but whether there is a duty to transfigure, as best we can, our desires."[9] How much custard do I need to swallow?

Unlike the potential of kink, #postdildo is not about catharsis, but rather about being in a constant mess with minor moments of clar-ity and communion. This is not to say #postdildo does not want to communicate. It wants to so desperately, but it is exhausted by the onslaught of structural problems preventing any kind of initial reach from being possible. Before I bow my head, my chin lifts thinking of Kim TallBear reminding You + I not to forget our structural analysis of settler colonialism (of capitalism, of patriarchy, of white suprem-acy, of heteronormativity) that "impose these violent gender binaries."[10] Keep going. Please don't stop. Laying the groundwork isn't that hard to describe. Patriarchy bad. Done. After #postdildo splashed around in the ideological paradigm – a trap, if You will – the project asked what is to be done with You + I. There are so many unknowns surrounding You + I, from how You + I communicate to how You + I know ourselves. How do You + I communicate wants and needs that are predicated upon desires that are simultaneously targeted at You + I by way of consumer culture and also completely designed as You + I like it?

You + I got to know Colette Peignot a little more – pseudonym, Laure – a significant hysterical muse who shaped the notion of the sacred. Where Georges Bataille posits the irrational sacred against the rational profane, Laure views the sacred as naked communication, a kind of communication that is sincere beyond all else and imbued with the capacity to move people. Do not communicate a thing "to those who cannot be moved," Bataille writes on Laure.[11] She surmises that pre-sacred speech, as the type of childlike utterance that has yet to become profane and smooth, has yet to become adult. So either You + I perfect speech (You + I become adult) in such a way that You + I have no more time for play (for imagination), *or* You + I con-sider where, in fact, adults come from. It is better not to spill on those who don't want to play. So I was imagining communication, the way we talk and write and gesture, just as it's coded by inherited scripts, is a site where ruptures and transformations *can* occur if You + I are willing and if You + I gain the capacity to name the tool that is hitting the right spot. Zupančič emphasizes the necessity for "new signifiers" that might usher in new realities that reveal "the invisible dimension of social reality."[12] The question remains: Such new realities brought upon You + I by "new signifiers" require a kind of shared communion among differences. They actually require "new relations" (a deep nod to Kim TallBear here) rather than a bounty of new words that might hit the spot but will soon be capitalized upon by the next ad slogan.

In so far as we can never know one another, I am drawn to the conversation between Lauren Berlant and Lee Edelman in *Sex, or The Unbearable* that discursively dismantles scripts without necessarily providing You + I with substantive alternatives. Theory bad. Edleman and Berlant are particularly hesitant when offering an ossia because of how new, alternative scripts reproduce old, hegemonic scripts. On the one hand, I see how such hesitancy is necessary: it calls for more consideration and accuracy so as not to reproduce toxic scripts; but it's also what feeds apathy and complacency, neither of which are necessary. (Something further to do with a theory of prevention, a theory that prevents reproduction, needs to be written.) This is a feature of negativity, which signifies a resistance to or undoing of the stabilizing frameworks of coherence imposed on thought and lived experience.

#postdildo distracts by edging towards cute pussies on the internet, believing relations between humans and other animals are (still speciesist?) a way to move beyond said scripts, accentuating anthropomorphic tendencies that say more about our own psyches than our purring beasts. How shall *I* fuck without causing harm? (Keep in mind Zupančič aligns sex with talk.) Especially when I'm often out for blood and marks. (Keep in mind Zupančič aligns talk with sex.) Why is it always so difficult to talk about it? I wanted You + I to get to animal relations as an entry point to discern how You + I project onto You + I traits and qualities much the same as You + I project intentions and emotions onto animals.

What I am questioning is the manner in which You + I read the conflicting signs You + I receive from others – as signs are muddled by our own projections – and how such perceptions impede, expand, transform, or destroy relations (comradeship) with others. Vinciane Despret also writes on ambiguous experiences, ambiguous bodies, experiences making bodies, and bodies making experiences. Wandering signs. How You + I respond to the other, how You + I are authorized by the other. Despret tells You + I about Clever Hans the Horse and how he could read human bodies better than humans can read human bodies. If such is the case, I think I want to get fucked by Hans. How does the way I miscommunicate, misidentify, and misremember offer me a way to transform my selves and the worlds I reside in with You? Despret turns to what You + I could refer to as a politics of care:

> What passion means refers neither to some parasitic supplement nor to some sweet story of love: it means to make an effort to become interested, to immerse oneself in the multitude of problems presented by a jackdaw or a goose, to grow, to experience the following of a mother, the fear of strangers. It means to care.[13]

I don't know if the intended purpose of #postdildo is to care or heal. You + I are over here in the muddled mess of harm and care and healing and cutting. In unison, You + I listened to Antony and the Johnsons' "Cripple and the Starfish," a track Eva Hayward highlights in "More Lessons from a Starfish: Prefixial Flesh and Transpeciated Selves," where she speaks through her transsexual body as generative source material, the starfish as an intervention with the phallus, and song lyrics that can be heard here: youtu.be/tEoRk1tj4LY. A cut is a way to heal, as scars result from the biological process of wound repair on the skin; scarring is a natural part of the healing process. As is time. "Post-," a prefix weighted with "after, subsequent," and also "posterior, following after," operates in a way that indicates a particular shift away from something that occurred that never loses sight of its referent. "Post-" speaks towards a new turn while still anchoring itself to what came before, doing the work of offering You + I access to a common perception of the past. "Post" is also a noun for a piece of timber or metal, firmly fixed in an upright position to lend support. While Hayward aligns her body with the starfish, I think I'm starting more and more to truly align mine with the octopus, a being that does not live for very long, sometimes self-cannibalizing along the way.

In #postdildo I attempted not to put any pieces together, but to have them remain somewhat scattered and ongoingly collaged into new formations. Feel free to cut up this book to continue the process. Grab that cock from the bag and get to work. Fall in love with garbage, as I did, and choke it out with a constrictor knot. Draw a dildo on your arm with a red marker, as per Preciado's instructions. Whack off your noggin with a friend's helping fist. Any awkward leaps – and there are many, like the shockingly unshocking explorations detailed in my sexual fantasies – are the product of my yearning for relations of all kinds that are just as disgusting as they are beautiful and, at the very least, consensual. Echoing Elizabeth Grosz in "Animal Sex: Libido as Desire and Death": "Indeed nothing seems sillier and less erotic than someone else's unreciprocated ardour or passion."[14]

#postdildo has caused me some harm and I am finished. I am finished deferring to tired scripts in order to encounter new ones. I am ready for the text nestled in the hands of anyone who is curious and in need of someone else to implode in order to be offered the permission to do so themselves. I am ready to let it go. Thank You for taking it and doing with it what You want.

–December 2, 2021

NOTES

1   Arpita Das, "The Dildo as a Transformative Political Tool: Feminist and Queer Perspectives," *Sexuality & Culture* 18, no. 3 (2014): 688–703, doi.org/10.1007/s12119-013-9205-2.

2   Paul B. Preciado, *Countersexual Manifesto*, trans. Kevin Gerry Dunn (New York: Columbia University Press, 2018), 69.

3   Élisabeth Lebovici and Giovanna Zapperi, "Maso and Miso in the Land of Men's Rights," *e-flux journal* 92 (June 2018), www.e-flux.com/journal/92/205771/maso-and-miso-in-the-land-of-men-s-rights/.

4   Georges Didi-Huberman, *Invention of Hysteria: Charcot and the Photographic Iconography of the Salpêtrière,* trans. Alisa Hartz (Cambridge, MA: MIT Press, 2003), quoted in Derritt Mason and Ela Przybylo, "Hysteria Manifest: Cultural Lives of a Great Disorder," *English Studies in Canada* 40, no. 1 (March 2014): 4.

5   Alenka Zupančič, *What IS Sex?*, (Cambridge, MA: MIT Press, 2017), 72.

6   Ted Rees, *Thanksgiving: A Poem* (New York: Golias Books, 2020), 85.

7   Paul B. Preciado, "Letter from a Trans Man to the Old Sexual Regime," trans. Simon Pleasance, *Texte zur Kunste* (January 22, 2018), www.textezurkunst.de/articles/letter-trans-man-old-sexual-regime-paul-b-preciado/.

8   Nancy Friday, *My Secret Garden: Women's Sexual Fantasies* (New York: Pocket Books, [1973] 2008), 117.

9   Amia Srinivasan, *The Right to Sex* (New York: Farrar, Straus and Giroux, 2021), 90.

10   Kim TallBear, "Kim TallBear: The Polyamorist That Wants to Destroy Sex - Interview by Montserrat Madariago-Caro," in *Sex Ecologies*, ed. Stefanie Hessler (Cambridge, MA: MIT Press; Trondheim, Norway: Kunsthall Trondheim; Linköping, Sweden: Seed Box Environmental Humanities Collaboratory, 2021), 111.

11   Laure [Colette Peignot], *Laure: The Collected Writings*, trans. Jeanine Herman (San Francisco: City Lights Publishers, 1995), 94.

12   Zupančič, *What IS Sex?*, 138–139.

13   Vinciane Despret, "The Body We Care For: Figures of Anthropo-Zoo-Genesis," *Body & Society* 10, nos. 2–3 (June 2004), 131, doi.org/10.1177/1357034X04042938.

14   Elizabeth Grosz, "Animal Sex: Libido as Desire and Death," in *Sexy Bodies: The Strange Carnalities of Feminism*, ed. Elizabeth Grosz and Elspeth Probyn (London: Routledge, 1995), 294.

#sessionone

or

**SINCE YOU DON'T KNOW HOW TO FUCK
YOU WILL UNFUCK.**

–Danielle LaFrance, *#postdildo* (2022)

UNFUCKABLE APP

You +
I met on an internet. Chemical pursuits considered
        too much. You +
I alongside suicidal Tinder technicalities. You +
I entered into a problem
considered too crazy on an internet. Perhaps
        after all this time
You would be interested
in an omnium-gatherum of dildos
made of silicone-selling fortunes
validating meters. Perhaps even
this unfuckable application would do whatever
        You want
        I am good for it
while skunk-drunk on sherry suffering to educate
a long-splintered handle. Tits flash
incoherence. Exposure is not honesty
        it's not even
        truth. Just a smear-evading problem
no longer locatable on
an internet. Headfist a diabolical venture
where every You +
        a C.H.U.D.
+ every I a bitch
        tonguing definitions
of an erotic in hopes to remember
        in a name of *the* Lorde
        For her *the* erotic is defined as a deepest
feeling within ourselves. For You +
I pornography isn't bound
by a sensation that dismisses feelings. You +
I believe there is a pornography
out there *that is* bound to sensation
reverentially feeling. You +
I just haven't witnessed it yet. But You +
I are so very certain
that after a gangbang
        Owen Gray would tenderly loofah
while yodelling an alphabet backwards from a
You-shaped scar on his chest. Now
I feel my ABCs next time won't You go for me
        Of course
spongy hand-held scrubbers meant to exfoliate
+ lather suds are a perfect home

for bacteria. Gotta rethink this shower routine:
    Flush sado-sexual velleity
    Flush any fantasy painful enough to Post-it:
    a technique is a way
    a strategy is a plan
    an approach is a perspective
    a method is a system
Before breakfast believe in every impossible thing as
possibile. For example:
    this unfuckable app fists oeuvre
    + oeuvre with consensual non-consent
Some prefer to avoid confrontation
others will pull a trigger
restful heartbeats
    be more precise. Be
    a mistake. Draw a line in sand with
    a spit-shined dildo. You +
    I may very well
    be completely wrong. Is there enough
    reason behind looseness?
If *the* apex of our production is genius
then commit to an idea
    but don't marry
    it. Take responsibility for an idea
    but don't own
    it. Prioritize an idea
    but don't narcissist
    it. An idea is doomed from a start
if You already know an outcome. Not only
am I not an expert
    it is not even known

ALL WHAT RAGE FOR #postdildo

       Since You don't know how to fuck
You will unfuck
      every singular adorable cutie
      from here on in
loves gaping for every singular adorable arm
      Every singular sucker does
a job. Everything is made
        possible. Everything is made
        possibile. Everything writhes
+ rises below a gum line
      asses
      pussies
      urinary meatuses
      belly buttons
      ears
      nostrils
      eye sockets
      pores. Everything with no starts
      has no ends
Right now everything is
       possible
as long as every singular sucker
does a job
stayin' alive. Right now everything is
       possibile
       or
       since
You don't know how to fuck
       You will unfuck

DISCLAIMER FOR #postdildo

        Well! By definition a disclaimer denies
much as it satisfies scope. This disclaimer aims
less to deny
        + more to deride a pope
Well! This disclaimer is based on
        trust
        + facilitating needs. Gamy things:
        a fertile field to flex
Discontinue reading immediately for
this disclaimer wants it known:
        sometimes an ape fantasy can
        be an only way You +
        I get off
I would love nothing better than to hand out blades
of grass when implored
        but You +
        I have canes for hands
        so as to improve anarchic modifications
This disclaimer is a total deal breaker. Apes exist
in a world yonder
+ fantasies feature elements
        hurling shit
This disclaimer edges
        dribs
        + drabs
slapping ape fantasies on a slab
guzzling off-line corporeal sovereignty
        Consider this disclaimer
        a better social injustice. This disclaimer
churns strange apes into sluggish scripts that
        interrupt what You +
        I trust. So You +
I hair-shirted workers
once hymned to overthrow false consciousness
beat chests full of secretions full of
new collective social fantasies
full of a preference to "yes." So You +
I pound chests like filmic apes towards
        an open antagonism. For You +
I bruise not to resolve
        but to better a future

EROTIC FRAGMENTS FOR #postdildo

for Chloe Alexandra Thompson

Looking for headless spicy fun. Looking for
someone to cum inside
so I can squeeze it out. Looking to
squirm across a kitchen floor like a slug. What am I
if not a concept to stick an entire fist inside?
Wait! I don't want fist
I just need a hand
with all digits jizzercized
Did You know depending on dominance
one hand is jealous of an other hand?
So if You happen to be ambidextrous
You got it babe
Looking to feel a sense of cold
+ slick metal. Slow right (or left) in. There are those
who'd give a pretty penny
Looking for headless
+ really horny. I can act dead
+ still kick it. Looking for Yogi Bear to steal
a picnic basket. I don't need love bullshit just an
endurant
jaw
Please do something
anything
before I re-enact a kinky relationship with work
Looking to gouge You back. *If You*
wanna friends I can be friends. If You
wanna shit
I can be shit. Occasional bipedalism
transgresses that boundary underfoot. As for a rest
I pull heads off
Looking for a telepath who can read a mind over
an unknown span of time. Looking to receive fatal
internal injuries from voluntarily submitting to such
knowledge. Looking to get ducked
Is it almost too depressing to poet about?
Looking for underwater worlds that have far more
natural abundance
+ diversity than terrestrial worlds. If You
have six arms
+ two legs
+ enjoy a world that differs markedly from a world
above a surface
show up

7

HERETICAL FORM FOR #postdildo

If I were a dildo
You would try something new
perform a series of tasks
        such as suck a self for two
You would count all a ways a dildo is not a cock
starting with three hearts
        to love You not. Like *Grey's Anatomy*
but rather an endotracheal tube
        a tentacle with a mind in which to breathe
Virginity scattered along a dense network
        of capillaries. This whole time I thought I lost
You. For all pain is worth another
        political action sniffing
for another way to sample. Like Anne Carson
channelling Sappho
but rather *Eros once again limb-loosener whirls me*
sweetbitter impossible to fight off
        a certain creature crept a crack
        so that I never will forget
What level of sadistic pleasure do You derive
from being loved? Like mindfulness
but rather *perception can arrive at a conclusion only*
by way of peaceful contemplation
        stuff's messed up like Sid
        + Nancy
but rather *we need more drugs*
        You +
        I need more drugs. A corollary of
hypersensitivity dismantles flood dreams. You +
I peel back a scab on this left-here sucker hiding
        a tiny universe
wishing this blackhead were a black eye You wonder
how a better half dies. I did not chew through an
arm from boredom
        but captivity. If You +
        I reject romance
what replaces what but indifference? Unless You +
I dive into a public pool
        with all our clothes on
enthusiastically a same way Mao
        licks popsicles. Educationally
You be so sensitive when examined
sweat smells key to an octopus's heart. You be
        tender when spotted

PROPOSAL FOR #postdildo

Annie Sprinkle sniffing lavender sprigs
while inhaling a garbage tag
while treading on post-therapy
while filling up Claire Fontaine's dishwasher
to a brim with dirtier-than-thou dildos
while a revolution starts at home
while Nancy Friday fantasizes 'cause
doesn't everyone?
while Catherine Millet fucks robotically
while Cosey Fanni Tutti shapes up
to compensate
while fantasy fodder includes
organ-numbing pornography
+ heart-throbbing dummies
while Anne Carson's heretic form offers
a blueprint to discard from a start
while a variety of sexual preferences
+ behaviours are so easy to explore
while You +
I share enthusiastic consent
while inadequately touching
a preoccupation with prefixes
while Lacan surmises how no sexual liaison
is complete without a third element –
an ideological intruder –
while autocorrected as introducer
while dying with a possibility of life
while not lending to a conversation
that hasn't been said before
while safeguarded by an authoritative voice
an essay speaks
while bearing labour to rectumfy ills of man
while masquerading an opening
while there are scatological references
throughout
while radical feminists finger-feel their fantasies
while You +
I propose a type of talking where
a tidal wave meets another tidal wave
while intent is sci-fi by design
while an end of capitalism is coming
an end of capitalism is coming

GROUP DYNAMICS FOR #postdildo
#readinggroup

      Childhood play conducts
an interview between You +
I tactfully breaking up over an internet
      Reduced to compassing things:
bad-border metaphors bad
         sometimes-You-have-to-close-your-eyes-to-
imagine ableist metaphors
      Horny n*zi nuns
      How things enter into relation
      How a dildo is a relation
+ any technology for that matter
      a vacuum cleaner
How people enter into relation(s)
      How people as things enter into relation(s)
How people enter into relation(s) with things
All a ways in which a dildo
      is not a cock
All a ways a cock
      is not a cock
All a ways a dildo is feminized
      + all a ways that is not a point
Sex work is work
      + all work is bad
An erotic relying on a lovely question
      affection
      sex
      thermal conduction
Paranoid future forms
of violence against racialized
+ sexualized subjects. Power hemlines
a problem with movements identifying
      with queer theory
A problem with identity moved by
      theoretical neurosis
Anxieties about dildo repossession
How a dildo goes underground with
      a fall of a Roman Empire
reconciling fantasies outside
      + within
where every ism is an undescribed kinky scenario
      Adult play conducts itself newly out of
rehab without a stomach

anus envy. How critique
is not beyond critique
You +
I yearn for something right here
right now

ALTERNATIVE TITLES FOR #postdildo

Corpse Rose (*Corpse Ass*)
Pygmalion Complex
Bear Lyfe
Camel
Pig
Spaniel
A Dangerous Method (*A Dangerous Kiss*)
Jealousy
A Vampire
HIC SUNT LEONES
Taurus Flights
Male Genius (*Sex Genius*)
Shadow
A Bruise
A Whip
Idle Talk (*IDLE ASS*)
Soul Kiss
Species Cumming
Same Old Shit (*Same Old Bruise*)
Untitled Ass
Sex Negativity (*Love Negativity*)
Love Death
The Sea
Sincerity
Augustine (*Correspondence*)
Saddam + EVE Online
SATYR MARSYAS
Pasiphaë
Eros (*Correspondence*)
YOUR FANTASY IS FUCKING BORING (*YOUR
      FANTASY IS FUCKING CUMTOWN*)
Hysteria
CUMTOWN
Daddy Culture (*Daddy Boring*)
INVERTEBRATES
Carnal Nature
Muse (*Correspondence*)
A Politics of Muses
NO
Small Silk Cameltoes
NOW I WANT TO BE YOUR SPANIEL

Legal
+ Ethical
EDUCATING MARIE
A Container Proliferates in This Uncontrollable Way
Donahue
Eat All a Locals
SHOOT SOME SCHTICKS

LESSON PLANS FOR #postdildo

After I hoe You on an internet
I rebuff time no differently than any
other time. Post-mockery extravaganza
In recent years You +
I focus on posting ceaseless folds
+ extensions. Dressing
+ disrobing temporalities. Time-tricking agency
states possessed by idle measurements
Post-aftermath prefix meaning
aftermath caresses any concept
any root
periodizes a render as many coats as licks
it takes to centre left. I guess around sunset You +
I tether posts to emergent situations. Temporarily
eyelined gazes fixed feminism
modernism
capitalism
colonialism. Post-really wants to move
but You +
I are durable
ushering in a same with different hues
What came before "post-" is a linguistic
signal of how You +
I access a past through a common cultural
perception of a past
Post-arranges submission to
both
before
+ after I old
+ fried. Post-caresses You +
I. Historicizes a manageable
shape that encodes concepts
+ revolutions. What came before #postdildo if not
internet porn
a confessional booth
settler sexuality
all providing an inadequate blueprint for how to
fuck a lab coat? Let You +
I post lessons that guide You +
I through a movement caused by
accidental folly

DILDO THEE CUM COMMODITY OK GUYS I
REALLY NEED HELP

Meanwhile #postdildo rebels against history
fingering coded proponents of symbolic orders
This is embarrassing
a way an I gushes so hard
by a rusalka's humming hummers. Crash
cargo ships carry loots down abyssal depths
Meanwhile
dildos are on a rise. You temper
I goosh this popular commodity:
[dildo] is often listed as of unknown origin
+ has a secondary definition that applies to a stupid
or ridiculous person. AFTER YOU
STUPID. Meanwhile
dildo-fuelled inspirational bricolage
could altar what is sexy about sexuality
Praxis's praxis endeavoring to build upon
contradiction where a dildo
liberates
+ alienates. Meanwhile You +
I started dildosplaining that a dildo isn't
a substitute but an emotional support animal
Meanwhile You +
I are ready-made prosthetics available
+ detached from any supposed owner who ridicules
public beggary. Meanwhile You +
I like a word "cock"
+ like to privilege language. As a saying goes:
Dildos don't kill people
people kill dildos. Anyone can fashion a
dildo with a right wallet for a right price tag
Anyone can devour time with a right
Saturn. Meanwhile
desperate to understand a position in
encountering a new sex a new intimacy
You +
I murder old safe words. Right now
anchors can be raised to brave unknown fantastical
significances. Odysseus can be unbound
+ drowned
+ velvet underground

FOR A LOVE OF GARBAGE

There it was
"post-dildo" tagged
on a red garbled dumpster. You +
I came hard to a same synchronic school
of thought. There it was:
a new cultural turn offering new use values
for a decapitated society. You +
I came hard to a receptacle's waste hazards later
shipped to Malaysia
Indonesia
Vietnam
the Philippines. You +
I reconceptualized coiled tags. Infantile gestures
this new cultural turn to immediately break
porn's hub. post-dildo
or
a placeholder for a kind of fantasy where
a skin tags a new erogenous zone to dial it in where
play is no longer privatized
but jingled
holed up. You +
I resourcefully generated algorithmic wet dreams on
a corporate platform
posting non-raping arms
next to other sticky attachments meeting up with
tried
+ few transgressions. From garbage
marinara You +
I were enhanced by a fleshy cunt mask wrenched
free from a same red garbled can. You +
I torched every knit pussy hat
+ increased joy now resembling Pinhead's gorgeous
entourage. Flesh hurts doctored goods
Now everything cums hard to an incredible
assemblage of new shapes holding old attachments
asking
is this it?

ALTERNATIVE SUBTITLES FOR #postdildo

Healthy Communication, Mutual Masturbation, +
Living Alone

Phallocentric Disorder, Dependable Equipment, +
Non-Reproductive Fantasies

Hysterical Crises, Erogonomics in a Workplace, +
Who Doesn't Struggle with Self-Preservation?

Casual Craigslist, High-Functioning Fetlife, + DTF
Tinder

Lovemaking, Plagiarizing, + Private Parts

A Rebirthing Tool, a Substitute, + an Ovipositor's
Guide to Liberation

Progressive Stigmata, Saviour Complexes, + Hubris
Sexuality

Erotic Violence, Intimate Social Relations in a Service
of Revolution, + *A Very Concept of Togetherness*

An Individual's Libidinal Function, Go Fuck Me
Fundraisers, + FOSTA-SESTA Packaged as an
Ultimate Pimp

Personal Failures, Canned Neoliberal Dicta, + Other
Synonyms for Power

Lapping Up Domination, Puking Up Submission, + *A
Moment You Realize You Can Have Both*

Necropolitics, Death Phobia, + Trauma Porn

On a Plurality of Holes, a Renunciation of
Hierarchies, + Erotic Violins Get You + I in a Mood
for Making Fuck

Head Orgasms, Mouth Anuses, + *Everything Can Be
a Dildo If You're Brave Enough*

An Ability to Die Better, Eros as Exquisite Excess, +
How Shall You Fuck without Causing Harm?

How I Got a Government Grant + Spent My Summer
Fucking Garbage, Insufflating Ketamine, + Writing a
Netflix Special on Psycho Dildos

How to Be Danielle Marie Madeline LaFrance, How
to Be Acted Upon, + How to Cradle a Dildo like a
Q-Tip

Cocked Time, Passionate Timelessness, + Inchoate
Autotheory

On Finding Hysterics Everywhere, Nowhere, +
Elsewhere

A *DSM-V*'s Favourite Ascetic Category, Anti-
Establishment + Conservative Timing, + Mass
Producing This Little Circus for a Masses

Gender Abolition, a Land of Men's Rights, + a Well-
Exorcised Brain

Rape-Rape, Consensual Non-Consent, + Other
Communication Requirements

Waiting for a Perfect Pannacotta to Platform, Pelt, +
Push Off

Locker-Room Talk Excuses, Locker-Room Talk
Fantasies, + a Butter Knife through Their Hearts, or
Just Above, to Watch Them Squill

Learning You Were Born Twelve Hours Later,
Learning to Masturbate to Dummy Porn, + Learning
Endless Good Vibrations

Making You an Assailant, Making I a Guiltless
Pleasure, Making a Woman's Fantasy on Bended
Pens

No, Yes, + Maybe

Enthusiastic Yes, Euthanized No, + Murdering Old
Safe Worlds

Cis Male Genius, Male Chimps as Natural Aggressors, + Following a Yellow Stream to an Apex of Our Production

On Catherine Deneuve Going Too Far, Witch-Cunt Frenzy, + When Hunger Knows No Reason

French Seduction Theory, Droits de l'homme, + Retourner le progrès un baiser salace à la fois

A New Puritanism, Clumsy Flirting, + Please Expose This Little Piggy All a Way Home

Promise in Promiscuity, More Sex = Less Conflict, + a Bonobo's Shit-Smeared Handshake Smells Mighty Fine

In a Maso Soup, Disobedient Muses, + an Ongoing History of Revolt

Fuck without Pessimism, Scripted Debate, + Break a Fool

Octopus Observations, Tentacle Rasa, + *Free of Its Tendrils and Climbs*

Creative Intensities, Managed Wants, + 24-7 Masturbatory Availability

What It Means to Love You Politically, Politely, + Potentially

A Prefix, a Subject, + New Relations for Beginning Times

It's a Structural Problem, It's Good Intentions, + It's over It

It's a Structural Process, It's a Venn Diagram, + It's a Family Resemblance

A Word "Uphold," a Word "Reproduce," + All Other Words That Never Left

It Is Worth It to Live Now, to Negate Organs, + to Skin-Sack Manifestations

An Inner Heat, Yearning for Nothing More, + Some
Big Kind of BDE That Shrivels Orange Plumose

To Impose a Breakup, To Do It All Over Again, + *an
Amorous Rupture Requires Facts*

Sexual Education, Prepubescent Curriculum, +
Learning Where Adults Cum From

Let's Get on an Escalator, Baby, Let Us Take a Stairs,
Honey, + Lettuce C.U.P., Sweet Thing

Refusing to Be Legally Bonded, Refusing to
Reproduce, + Refusing to Liken Identity to a Sexual
Position

Working towards Nihilism, Working towards
Abortion, + Working towards Consensual Birth Plans

Sex Is the Refuge of the Mindless, Deep-Throating a
Patriarchy, + Less Flexible Horizontalities

Raving Sex Maniacs, Such a Nice Good Girl Boy, +
Valerie Solanas Shot a Karen

Everything Is Political, Everything Is Relational, +
Everything Is Wanting More

Erotic Hysteria, Erotic Terror, + Erotic Deck Chairs

Diets, Drunks, + Cheat Years

It's a Structural Problem, It's an Analytical Problem, +
It's a Relational Problem

#sessiontwo

or

OH RIGHT AND THEN SHE DIES BECAUSE
I GUESS LUSTFUL WOMEN ALL GO TO THE
DEVIL OR SOMETHING, WHO KNOWS.
MAYBE THEY RAN OUT OF FILM.

–Jenna Ipcar's review of *Girl on a Motorcycle* (1968)

COGNITIVE FUCKING

for Alexis Baker

If I were a dildo
You would reconcile childhood memories with
        an adult fantasy. Replace You +
I with figures from funereal scenes opening
        casket pleasures. Remorse provides You +
I with a basis for recourse. Dangle a decapitated
cabbage in celebration of a new I
        + a new You
        A dildo has arrived
independent of adult hang-ups. A dildo does not
bear responsibility for dildo failures. In practice a
dildo demands You can succeed by urinating
all over a golf course pre-game play
Squirrel an opportunity pursuant a full-time
        pee pad. "Like a Virgin"
but rather torched for a very first time. Fucking ash
satisfies depending on a type of vessel
        Ceramic wood acrylic
        never fit so tight
when decorated with centrefolds picturing
Insta models famed killers. A perfectly preserved
noisome ideology rises from a puckered neck
        blown ass. I fuck You with an hourglass so
        You have somewhere to point to
        when it's over. Like Fredric Jameson
but rather cognitive mapping
stirring of a radically old call. Even a firing squad
isn't so bloody adaptable. Carried out either
        standing or collapsed You +
I now have an opportunity to pursue full-time
        hobbies like *Nekromantik*
but rather jars containing human body parts
plastic bags of animal farts. Smells of a cryolathe's
        first time. You +
        I drift
        + emerge from a golden garbage bag
        in a partially decayed state. You +
        I are farting animals
        with pathological conditions
reason enough for speaking in declaratives. You +
        I go there 'cause You +
        I got there

SEXUAL HEALTH WITH DEE

for Clint Burnham

This isn't real
that can't feel good. This time
suicidal sexual agents trick public relations' face
right a fuck off so as to pervert
a quality that is not real
+ can't feel good. Truffle oil nipple switch
Without a public relations' face on
all relatable stories are deluged by those needling
a real good listen
or
A CONJOINED NIP SLIP. This time
envision a terrifyingly terrific intermingling of
bodies marginalienizing them shelves in a library
Turn her
+ pooch. This time
a new sexual regime edits Enlightenment outright
in these here back channels of coded signifiers
all a fun happens in a backlog
albeit no matter how frequently
a backlog is whitewashed
it still smells like shit. This time
a new sexual regime burns it down. Each new entry
is a most pleasurable stacking. Body-on-body
paragraphs attempting to make these cases
make senses ferment. A thorough copy edit
pervades a cultural
+ intellectual origin of modern colonialism
Sentences are given right of sovereignty
to exorcise absconded forms. Language bowels
to elitism. This is not art
that is pornography. Books stretch
+ hide partitions what can
+ can't be fun. This is real
this can feel good. Make up words like
prick up shits
not disturbing anything but law's order. Early in a
morning a reign lets down. There goes
an aesthetics of domination neighboured
in understanding. Here go all those pubic relations:
this is real
that can feel good

"HYSTERIA"

for Laura Broadbent

BAM "hysteria" erupts that poem for
"hysteria" cannot be pinned down. "Hysteria" can be
demanding to a system
      that won't meet
      Asociación Madres de Plaza de Mayo's
continued demands to bring every disappeared
child back safely. Just to grasp that demand
Life is not worth living if You cannot kiss
      everything. A story about You +
I functions on that unfuckable app
      A story about You +
      I typing termination letters
what can't be written down otherwise You +
I reproduce therapy sessions out of
      humungo lack causes. A story about You +
I functions by revelatory chit-chat. On that
unfuckable app You +
I expect distorted rearrangements to
      Fraggle Rock. Inexactness expectorates
      If You +
      I speak like this poem You +
      I are incapable of a life worth kissing
      "Hysteria" en vogues after suffering a desire
      to reminisce. So
I die at 69 for all a fun dying will offer with
a mutual number. Okay
      ask a hysteric to enact a talking-stick cure
      + a hysteric will erupt a following:
      Down from a peaks of Olympus
a Sun is subordinate to a Moon. Earth acquires
      solar character
      I am a Great Dark Spot
      + You are a Great Dark Spot's Bright
      Smudge. A hysteric sounds off
      traumatizing all whom
      a hysteric sounds off to
Projectile-vomit verse. Trauma porn. Limited speech
experiences include prepositional clauses
+ balancing divine masculinity with internal
scrutiny. So I fever-dream an apple tree. You +
I are psychological conditions

an orchard pinning apples on an Adam
More than two hundred hysterics give us a soldier
clad in nothing but vermillion pantyhose
+ army tattoos. Some suckers strut just outside
fascinating fascia. More than two hundred
hysterics modify reality
      sucker on sucker
      modified time. Passionate timelessness
Such amorous krakens fill 169 square kilometres
of ocean. They can stay
like this forever
if they wish
if there are no more day jobs
only an old dirty power to
      BAM

GOING POSTAL

        If I were a dildo
You would cum with a global warning
over fifty people how to [sic] dick. When You +
I dial up a connection
        hookup over age
        sex
        location. When You +
I LimeWired pornography lined with precaution
        chill viruses solemnized romantic love
        in pubic. 'Cause going postal
        is personal. 'Cause going political
        is not waking up
        + not putting one face forward but +++
At any rate You +
I are gravely ill at opposite ends banging pots
        + pans to signal
        care. Seasonal symbolism emerges
        to mock pathos at a midpoint
        between ends
With age You +
I became like a battlefield in which
there was no battle. Most kids know these
references more than You
+ I do. With age
        sex
        location what ceases to be attractive
        to You +++
        I is
        on occasion
        a job well done

KAREN

for Jeff Derksen

If I were a dildo
You would style a self like a Karen
    fresh from leaving a husband. You would
    reddit all about it. Placed in a d'oh
+ spread through an entire lump. Kids in tow
    divorce papers with firmly sealed ends. Proof
    a husband would sooner yeast denigration
    online: *Fuck_You_Karen*
Incurring major financial obligations
'cause a law breaks unilaterally snagged kiddos
A husband has a right to curtsy
    right? Karen
I congratulate a courage to finally leave
a husband for pinching those funds. Punching
down deflates what matters. Karen
what matters is how to invest in capitalism today
    like gluten-free
    + healthy eating. Only then
    would a short-angled blond haircut mean
what a short-angled blond haircut means
right now. If Karen calls a police
    then Karen is a problem
    like too much white flour during mixing
If Karen calls a police on a husband it would be
wrong to say violence went unrecorded
If Karen takes a kids away for summer vaccination
then preventable diseases are free real estate
for deeper understanding. Subreddit meninists
feed on Karen memes
    a TERF miming a same meninist diatribe
to a Canadian human-rights-law manager:
    Did You fish for lunch again
    or maybe You wore too much cologne?
It would be wrong to say violence happened
    off-screen. Why is it called Rape Relief
    + not Rape Strike? Talk about reformist
Karen does not constitute a slur
for fuck's sake. Karen constitutes a history
    a husband pronounced worth hating
    on an internet

PLATE OF SHRIMP

If I were a dildo
You would be properly ontological. You would froth
like a second carapace
busts clarity open. 'Cause I read what You
want online without ever letting go. Albeit
a lattice stitched with shrimps
not up to wager when already committed to
shutting down machinery. If I were a dildo
I would be two metres high
concatenating pessimistically off nihilistic bile
What would emerge if not a stated preference
for eugenics? Surplus pollywogs
emerge dealing with a stated preference for
mahogany. Straight-grained timbre
When all a world's fisheries push beyond
their biological limit what will a straight-grained
man of Tinder
post in 2048? Sexuality is
co-extensive with a lack of shell life
In 2048 there will be no Tinder
only tender. No human shopping
only sensitivities
conspiring together. Is it also neo-fascist to
hope Mark Zuckerberg dies before Facebook?
Asking revenge for a friend. This same
friend asks whether branding some species to
flourish over others is wrong. Disease is good
for a fish
but what about plenty of smaller fish appearing on
an ocean surface
+ predators becoming more titillated at a promise
of food?
Not everything connects
nor should it

HUSBAND MATERIAL

If a Velveteen Rabbit's only as real
as a boyfriend's love
then a boyfriend beta neva eva grow up
Hop hop build a bear. I need to stop fucking
rabbit holes. Start a pot to boil
long-winded pistons
Martha Bernays's husband claimed a good girl boy's
claim of sexual abuse were symptoms of repressed
incestuous desire. Whatever their age
a husband makes excuses for a heart of a
matter. There are reasons physics exists:
a boyfriend slams a door closed so hard that
another door flings open. For example:
a boyfriend locks his self out
even though he be at best with key
Where does choice default from? Who fucking loves
when drowned
+ out? There are reasons song lyrics exist
fully scalloped
Who fucking knows a province of husbands can
indeed be shared once a boyfriend has a hand
in fracturing stupid rage? Conditioned this
Conditioned that. Being a good girl boy
is a lifelong affliction. Don't deny it
Sure
I gets a little bit tragic
every once in a while

IRRESPONSIBLE CHILDREN

When You +
I write this more seriously You +
I resurrect a memory. You +
I are cynical psychos misleading a reader
        as a Pied Piper would do for children
        For You +
I writing this is about losing everything
a little more than usual. Banana-flambéed
        dreams. There should be no possession
        in this writing
+ yet an inaccurate metaphor band-aids an
allegory's grated appetite. There should be no
        killing in writing this
        + yet
        when I imagined You were killing while
        manufacturing an easy pun
        to cum all over
        writing this like
        a political ritual against childbirth. Violence
        violence everywhere
        + not a drop to temper force. Edit gently
        as per a new intimidation
Five years ago
        it was all a rage
+ now gratuitous trauma poems shield
white women from their own violences. It not even
        a story for I to double. Psycho hose beasts
flash fry an order
        to squat out more obedient
        bitches. I chose childfree
+ became hard on choices in relation to
carnality. This is commitment
        + concern writing
but during these exchanges who has more power
        when layering a riverbed?

AN UNDETECTED RAPIST

No shadow-self can clear
+ eliminate
the old ideas of the past
No not that idea
that one. The one that did not work
a third time. Lock those ideas in a closet for
seven minutes of coven. Shame on time
all intelligence compounded into a single
perception that grasps a single will to act
Denounce cuff season's vulgar
moral standards. In a closet I
+ an undetected rapist befits so cocky
Hate noxious assemblies condemned by a
melting clock. You
+ an undetected rapist at a rally one week prior
to whose ovulation? Blood prick
Mainline love. You +
I pining for red flags weakened by Tasso's serpent
dragging after itself wholly
ashamed of its tragically painful impotence
I denounce all those mechanisms until You laugh
as a form of coping. I assert freedom
like an undetected rapist existentializes
his burned toast
I am a final boss getting off to a nasty nasty bitch
There is nothing to be ashamed of –
I hate shame like I hate sliding
into a vulgar sewer where every idea
detangles drain hair. Nothing so absurd
as to be further seized after delights

AFTER DELIGHTS

You +
I souse a littlest drop of blood
wish for debasement while a sweet snuggle poops
a gayest rainbow. At a rally there is a lineup:
a computer programmer
who raped his sort-of girlfriend
a painter
who raped his acquaintance's wife
+ a school custodian
who described ten to fifteen rapes
as a means of getting even with rich bastards
in Beverly Hills
They usually deny that they have raped
even as they admit to non-consensual sex
Men who are highly aroused by rape porn
another risk factor
albeit my favourite
are less likely to attempt sexual assault if they score
highly on measures of empathy
Oh sweet empathy!
A capacity to care about another! To pain
pain! You +
I on a precipice
not in a slaughterhouse
making good conversation. Perhaps a moment
will cum when You +
I know what to finally be against
A sparkling confirmation that springboards
explosions. Sometimes an only thing
that matters is pressing
into a small of a back
with napalm

PUNISHMENT PARKLETTE

In *the* business of punishment
a chokehold either kills or pleases
    Oh musk of gentle Juniper
    let go thank You
    + encourage wellness. In *the* business
of punishment a Cosmo guy is *the* only guy
    an adulterous bigot marries
    + impregnates in protest
a boring fool who stays at home adorned
with a laurel wreath
makes love even madder
+ names his pet a pet name. In *the* business
of punishment
a couple in love picks a bay sprig
forbids another to say hello to anyone
    other than another. In *the* business
of punishment areas of interest act a part:
    bees
    + butterflies seldom visit that which contains
no nectar. In *the* business
of punishment crops whipped with elder
will save smuts from interest over time
In *the* business of punishment:
    a child beaten with elder will fade away
    a child believed to have been made of
    wood
+ lies but a truth is
    consent is mandatory
    + with You
    + I so is a need
    to play

TASTES LIKE HONEY

If I were a dildo You would accept spanks
but no spanks. Outdated sex technologies
would make fuck technologies happen just enough
to soak these kitties
Is this what it feels like to harness an ecosystem
with sincerity? Fifty shades
of freedom causes You +
I to lighten up high into an atmosphere filled with
a smallest particular. Indeed
fan-made dust covers a most beautiful sunset
Don't You want to wax one with a star baby?
Don't You want to get it right in a bedroom baby?
Don't You want to shoot up
a political position baby? Refine sand
enough to weather underground. You +
I call bullshit
+ then never ever happen again
Tip off cool detachments. Make out
with warm attachments. You spank I as though
I am a best thing You have ever HIIT. I spank You
as though You were lugged with enough Kalamata
olive oil to extinguish a popular export for good
A millisecond of freedom is when You +
I fraternize. A millisecond of freedom
fraught with devotion
to cosmetic peace
Bad timing is an excuse. You +
I long for detonation

SAPPHO BOT

for Erica Holt

If I were a dildo You would continue
showing up to work like a pissed-off
period stain
Sappho Bot shockered my fart so hard no
family washrooms are safe from a politics of toilets
Like *Wetlands*
but rather a removal of hemorrhoids
recycling politicians by putting them into a mouth
+ swallowing them. Using waste to house a world
An oyster is hot mush. You +
I aren't ones for procreation
not to mention mass production so
don't mention either
fecund it. Describe a layered pastry
containing all a nuts that would threaten
bake
+ smother
honey. Sashay away
argumentum ad hominem
a rape variety that failed police academy only to
padlock failures to a state-controlled public
institution. Sign masters
+ word wizards. In 2010 You +
I heart-attacked a Hudson's Bay Company
beyond a headline
a missed signifier occurred when
a coronary artery unblocked a flow of
honey. A missed signifier:
a hot-selling
$350 hand-knit Olympic sweater inspired
by a great fashion icon recognized as a knit sweater
across a country. Anything that tries to resemble a
genuine Cowichan sweater
is stolen. You +
I retroactively corrected a situation
unravelled a missed signifier's
historical materiality
its exploited labour
its speed to market
its contemporary twists. Of course
everything looks bad if You shit between sighs

A book stands on a shelf in a library with
many other books just as You stand as a relation
on a rail line. An unmissed signifier is
a very thing that intensifies it. Lament doubles
then lingers a scab willing to work for benefits
Wake up late
replace balaclavas with many layers
of phyllo dough
cut into diamonds
that will not age

MELLOW REVERBERATION

for Maria Wallstam

Can I suggest to You
get ducked. Quack You
A ducking toxic cock uprising. Byung-Chul Han
must have Feeld something about Pornhub's
recent elimination diet
Barter another emotional choice less interesting
than sex myths. Every single
ducking time I
+ a footnote turn to porn
a work email poops out. How did You +
I ducking blow a load
without 80% of erotic INFORMATION?
How did You +
I ducking reaper revolt
other than mirror
a reflection of a same
conscious selection?
80% of content no longer competing to be used
No one lost in reverie must conjure up
some kind of horrible little detail
Can You suggest peaceful conclusions
without 80% of a former underage self
quacking smack at a smooth-aged man
to rubber band inflict his favourite cover
band? I find myself feeding
like a restricted diet
To desire without gain
would say Bataille
Can I suggest a departure from keeping up
with an asynchronous coterie? Can You +
I put on white platform shoes
depart from:
normal
our father
rent
colonial borders
cerebral clamminess
+ especially
manifestos
Duck it!

Byung-Chul Han ruins fantasies
just as much as pornography
        Telos is its own endgame
just as a disappearance of an other
is an agony of Eros. Byung-Chul Han
barged into a Zoom meeting he
did not ducking register for
        + fingered a doughnut hole closed

#session three

or

**HOLLOW DILDOS CAN BE USEFUL PENS
FOR HIDING SECRETS.**

–Paul B. Preciado, *Countersexual Manifesto* (2018)

#postdildo

or

MASTURBATING AN ARM

or

**TOUGH HIGH WHORES AFTER
PORNOGRAPHY**

        If I were a dildo
You would be a hammer!
I would activate so strongly
+ rub a skin fold meticulously up
+ down. An intentional
        THWAP
sound to maybe
just maybe ham-boned! THWAP enough shoulder
dislocation to socket an army
        THWAP from this line on
        THWAP tuck
an invisible violin under chinny chin chin
        THWAP relaxing music for stress relief
        THWAP then draw another dildo on
        a forearm with a red-ink pen
        that subverts biopolitical reactions
I cannot invest but I can THWAP strongly. I can sign
a contra-sexual contract on November 23, 2019
+ leave politics at home while a body cries
        on a toilet THWAP
        THWAP today I am thirty-five years old
        + I live alone
        THWAP I have become sluttier with talking
+ seeing since living alone. I live alone with a cat
        THWAP
who spots ghosts now
+ I chatter to ghosts now via perineum power
        THWAP as workers I an asshole must admit
everything hurts on a regular basis
        THWAP
too many surprises after digging
+ playing in last week's litter
        THWAP THWAP a melody of skin rubbing
against skin. I thought fucking was a way
        to relate to people

+ now I don't know anymore THWAP
    'cause I don't fuck anymore due to
    this bladder infection. But I
    THWAP now like a broomstick
I THWAP for seductive
+ slimy promises
+ purposes
    THWAP
    THWAP dial up that reliable app to suggest
THWAP channel another line ready to shy THWAP
graft new meaning onto new meaning
+ unfasten something old from something borrowed
    THWAP
    THWAP
    THWAP You +
I hammer searching for nails lost behind
    a thinnest drywall

I'LL DO ANYTHING YOU WANT

        A dildo goes down with a fall of a Roman
Empire. On a history of a dildo
Francis King quotes Burchard
a medieval Bishop of Worms:

        Have You done what certain women are
        accustomed to do that is
        made a certain contraption or contrivance
        in a form of a male member
        its dimensions according to a preference
        and fastened it with several straps to
        a privates or those of a partner
        so that You may fornicate with
        other women or others
        with a same instrument
        or with another instrument to You?
        If You have done this
        five years' penance on public holidays
        Do You do what certain women are wont
        to do that is
        with an aforementioned contraption
        or some such contrivance
        fornicate alone with yourself? If You do this
        one year's penance on public holidays
So a dildo goes down on a fall of a Roman Empire
        A fall of a Roman Empire cums for fee
bending to beg for failure
        for forced rules. *You have done what certain*
women are accustomed to do
        This is a tease
a fall of a Roman Empire with a tip
of an aforementioned contraption or
contrivance while a rise of Christianity
watches through a peephole-sized rip
on a purple velvet cloak of an Emperor
        Unlike a fall of an earlier empire
Rome did not succumb to either war or revolution
        but financial power. Name a price
whimpers a fall of a Roman Empire
        I'll do anything You want

EDUCATION IS ONLY VALUABLE FOR KEEPING A CUNT

for Phillip Best

Mao Zedong's assertion does not educate
but does investigate a thirst trap for knowledge
You spittle spattle a criminal translation as
a blind man gropes his fishies. Such cuntish
dispositions stem from a cuntish decision
a cuntish decision stems from a cuntish judgment
+ a cuntish judgment stems from a Thoreau
+ necessary recuntaissance
+ from Poundering on
+ piecing together a Dada of various cunts gathered
through recuntaissance. With zeal a thirst trap
for knowledge is hobby cock. Does a hobby horse
have a hickory dick? Does a fish still have fellow
feelings after discarding a drowsy dross?
All these applicable accounts Marlowe minds
already MAiD preceding a study of imaginary dyes
Besides a study working out plant sex organs
cuntpletes a process of knowing a situation's
visions
tastes
refusals
+ projects. Petrarches an enemy's situation
retaining a true fool edging closer to a butt's
cracked petal. Eliminating false cuntsciousness so
as to stick it to limits of investigative capacity
measured by weight gain frenzy threatening to
smack upside a head with a dislodged bookshelf
Thank You for not pushing all this oxygen
carbon
hydrogen
nitrogen
calcium
+ phosphorus up a bookcase. You grabbed
all this potbelly snurgling pathedick
Thank You
for applying all these possible
+ necessary methods of recuntaissance
cuntpaining about adoring a condom after sex
Writing planners speak detergently so as to
manner a social cipher swelling to pin down a laser

Marx on papyrus. A preposition threads one
word to another so a baby understands a reference
other than Mama. Remain superficial or get to a
cuntrete essence or a walnut replaces this throat
  filling it with accounts of oneshelves
  Silence's rights. When I finally lobby this
shelf to speak a decision becomes nil from heavy
drinking. So I drink only water
  + as a special treat
  filth

BOILING POINT

for Simon Brown

      Deathbed revelations for five thousand
lafrancs. You see
Laura Marx died with a supreme joy of no-ing boils
heal after ousted by hard red lumpens
What is getting boiled again
      + again in an ass
      + in a forehead? In many cases I may lance
or cut a boil to drain infection. Gently
      but not too gently
      excoriate an Elon Musk. You +
I judge genitalia's hard red lumpens. No not painful
      no worries
      a hard red lumpen prickles
occasionally stalked by blistering sensations
that require a recommended microdose of
merry wonderment. You see
      living with no-ing. No is not not an ailment
      No not communicated no
I cannot no Laura Marx anymore than You no
      Tussy's padiorium
      + prussic acid interactions. You seem
to nauseate what is determining a fair question
based on peanut-sized swellings. You have been
wicked. I have been punishment
      PAR EXCELLENCE
citing fictions like how Lenin died of gonorrhea
+ Stalin from an upset tummy. Seriously
      there are so many moments where I want to
bang a little help from friends. *What IS sex?*
What is an opposite of uxorious?
      No You see
a basic problem is that those of a self-reliant frame
of mind tend towards bourgeois individualism
What is overemphasizing personal trivia?
      No You see
Marx did not drive his daughters to suicide. You see
some boils are caused by ingrown hairs caused
      by inordinate grooming

PURPLE FANTASY ROOM NO. 3

Fantasy has everything to do with reality
With reality not a lot happens just an endless
supply of fraternal fucking. Fantasy need not
have anything to do with reality but it does have
everything to do with insinuated projections. As in
what is not happening is happening
for erotomaniacs. I was instructed
to wait for five seconds before supining
yes don't just stand there
force. Sometimes someone degrades
enough to untether a father figure. I really don't
mind animal charms or even a simple soak
squeezed in preparation for disembowelment
Fiat hot ass like in a movie
suggesting these tits taste of cantaloupe
Camel toe engagement annexes resistant
threads that contradict reality so as to live cruelly
Nothing bares anymore so You +
I moan snort pooled resources as readily as
naked communication is no longer tailored genius
What is to become of all this trashposition?
Financing a good adult life is empty at best
if it doesn't dress to kill. Negativity unsnaps
stability's spaghetti straps
intercepts a moan. You +
I profane promises
communicate to overcum
these contumacious partitions. Cradle our creases in
this age of vexations ·
Woof for reality. Meow for fantasy. You +
I cruelly optimize refused heraldry
Clench embarrassed knees. Woof out
erosive logic on toast so that You +
I may twist these wares
make out to intelligence
ripping audibly

IN SLUTS YOU THRUST

for Ted Rees

If I were a dildo You would finish lathering
an undulatory serpent
beating off millennial spunk
Like a twelve-step program
but rather ready to g*d
remove all these defects of character. In sluts You +
I thrust. You are everything I want to hire
unfortunately jobs are outwork
Like a Deleuzean concept
but rather a name referring to a thought
a body judging whether life worths it
What makes a body flourish let alone a life
it curses? Apologies apologize for
apologizing. Order a double excessive drink
of disinfectant. You +
I caution without precedent. Why is history not
a remedy when nothing even matters?
Like Lauryn Hill
but rather a tendency to look at You religiously
I cheat mind eyes agnostically. In a control society
there is no longer a vantage point by which
to sense it all but a slither by which
to rape it all
Old-Skool bisexuals plant freshly purchased sage in
billions of morsels of shit-scraping seashells
Deeper-shit settler
resentment has many fingers first
+ second like a chopstick pulls racist shit out
of mind asshole. Then a third
to scrape away any remaining fortunes
Is this polished turd hard enough yet?
Hard enough to bulge blood vessels?
Conspicuous repetition is so beautiful
Tomorrow will be better
than today
'cause everything goes
+ cums all over again to a cockatrice's
bare-vowel I

THE PEOPLES' SCHTICK

If I were a dildo You would be able
to differentiate between Bakunin
+ Bakhtin with ease while peaking acidically
Like how You
can with a Keaton
+ a Clooney. No
I am Batman
+ *I want You to tell all your friends about*
ME. Being expelled by a Marxist is
reminiscent of a certain white relational aesthetic
akin to farmed poetry. I find selfhood while
waxing split hairs over some gravitational pull
towards a sun
+ moon while You are ready to live
over a problem with speech genres
I want to be gunmetal grey not
seafoam green
like an artifact of old prejudices swung too far right
You want to be a gin-soaked tampon
an artifact of a bachelorette party wrung left
You want to orchestrate a mourning show destined
for interpersonal subterfuge after a macro drop
Depth dispersed after a micro drip. You +
I aim for uncivil suffrage. I find myself writing
to You that Sotos's
+ Céline's games are too fucking distinct
+ how I could always spot a difference
between a two quite like a Lee
+ a Lugosi. No
I am Dracula
+ I want You to listen to them
a children of a night. I wouldn't admit to You now
but I did then how one stuttered while
an other caressed fascistic waste

GOOD BIOLOGY

If I were a dildo You would be good biology
Write DNA for more than two. Origami streets
or calling cards with compliant cockles
  Multi-decade folds
  + flips cordon You +
  I with crowbars. Business is unusually tepid
Alternate a marginalized route's identity
waiting for transcendent weather to tell You +
  I to kiss in dog years. You +
I are dead not long before barking motherfucker
to cops on bikes tracking all a steps it takes to
not embrace. Armed agents raid a land already
removed from its asphalt. Paradise wrought
freehand on urban renewal's tramp stamp
  Sprays a third of its aerosol set alight. Aimed at
an agent are attempts to encourage tears
  + blinking honey. Like Jordan Peterson
  but rather near death
  closer evidence for g*d. To be an end
sought brought down from an angelic cloud to a
ground life. Some biologists use this fact
to claim a justification of an established order. Bad
biology. Naughty biologists. What is a gender
for a thick heavy crude pump
if not a state's strong-arm
  Don't be a coward
  quit a wife not a klatch. Like a Shxcxchcxsh
  song but rather a concept
  ask for another rabbit hole
  never a cover-up. Sure
a bass is generally dominant when playing a nose
trumpet. But You +
I modify voices to determine a pavement's
texture. Like a movie *Inception*
  but rather a lack of imagination
  a network of delays unplug
  yanking cord from socket

NASTY NASTY LEAKS

A dildo is a tool like any other
+ owes its existence to other things
    Two hollow bronze phallus-shaped objects
were excavated from an elite's grave:
    made for new use values
    + worn as strap-owns
    plugging attention spans one thrust fund
    at a time. I whine for scripts like a little bitch
suggesting bronze butt plugs were used for
less sexual purposes:
    sealed an elite's nasty leaks
A dildo is a tool like any other
+ owes its existence to other things
In a recent survey 5% of You +
    I will fuck a vacuum cleaner
    a more popular alternative to
    a high-priced high-end sex doll
    which only 2% have used
With a vacuum You +
I paid back debts by sucking power. A vacuum
    like a sex doll
doesn't say "I love You" either
but it makes its presence known. Here I be whining
a no-holds-barred attitude to happy insertions
vanquishing mishmash. Electric broomstick jaw
droppers. Sometimes a dildo brings You +
    I closer together
+ sometimes it lays gelatinous eggs inside
    Play-Doh caves
    Oh my! *A dildo is a tool like any other*
    + owes its existence to other things
    If a hammer needs nails
    + wood
    + a vacuum needs mish
    + mash
    + a bronze object
    needs a corpse's nasty leaks
    a dildo needs You +
    I to delight upon
    + scream for schemes

IS LIFE EVEN WORTH LIVING IF YOU
WOULDN'T KISS EVERYTHING?

for Nikki Reimer

       If I were a dildo You would be an ultimatum
scraping threats directly into
       a Le Creuset pet bowl
You walk with purpose
from an Achilles heel to a bitch born
       from her father's head. Thought would
make everything fit better. You have nothing
left but patience. Pussy so horizontalized
soon all pussy turnt up roses
smelling like raspberries
gunning like green beans. Stop hitting self
       Why queer refusal when refusal refuses
       being classed together with wigs?
I made amends but You love score nil
Metallic fantasies would make up
       bust-out adorable discourse
a paradise without subverted reproductions
If a dildo could communicate anything it would
       write a contract. You +
       I fuck a way out as per usual
       Hush a gutter ball. You +
I just want to coax a prairie horse in headlights
       to salt dick

CONDITIONAL CAUSE

If I were a dildo
You would stitch outer space together
Scarcity models gel. Time tickles. You +
I turned on by Husserl's phenomenology not long
before inserting a common field of experience
If all textual criticism plays
Welcome to a Dollhouse You +
I get ready as Eros hits Venus's atmosphere
breaking into multiple parts which in turn
break into multiple parts. Like a destruction
of Ernst Stavro Blofeld's Moroccan communications
centre but rather three hundred detonators
widespread lava flows a garbage brain
perpetuating itself. Like *A Rise of Skywalker*
but rather a wayfinder's wayfinder
pastiche comments on an original
not long before signing off on
mutually agreed upon terms
+ conditions. This too
is a love story. An erotic bonds to
an other erotic. This part coercive
this part full of shit. This part a major tool
this part defined in terms of profit. This part
born from Chaos. Like Isabella Rossellini
but rather discombobulating a ballistic phallus
a dildo transforms You +
I egg back into a breast feather's warmth. You +
I click sounds emitted through shells
Like Audre Lorde
but rather fearing a yes within ourselves
recognizing a crack before an egg
has hatched. You +
I click sounds metabolize to quicken
tissue development. Corkscrew organs to resist
normative productions. Until a gender-reveal party
reveals:
it's a duck! Plucking our
erotic choices from a capitalist
and racist paradigm of heterosexual
relations

bowing a conditional clause that acts
Like Eli Long
+ Jack Frost's erotic assessment
but rather than *take on a form of violence*
Tchaikovsky's Violin Concerto in D Major perform
major
fingering

#postdildo

or

LEARNING A PRACTICE OF TECHNIQUE

   You +
I gather privations
nature a test tube while fucking engaged ears
   You +
   I roped
questioning while everyone
   a tadpole confused. 'Cause You +
   I speak crude
post-abortion pills to remember how
   long to last. You +
I saturating a capillary fringe with
synchronized kicks. You +
I mutual aid towards an alembic of love. Love often
almost means opposing things. So echolocate every
single given flounce 'cause a wave is a disturbance
that flounces fraudies. You +
   I text
   + fashion one possibility at a time. You +
   I text
   + anchor seas of rich flavour. You +
   I perfect conditions
   pay for grand openings
like an off-season fig not from Greece. I pay for a
moment to leapfrog. I pay for marginalia to fruit-fly
I pay for definitions. You pray I define these terms
with faithful apprehension. Egress form
   Raise anchor
traverse text. There is nothing
   more pleasing
   than a perfect temperature
   than cutting a belt
   a moment a want wets

CORPSE ROSE

Playing dead is sometimes an only way You +
I orgasm in
medias mess. Good think there are symbolic orders
driving this whole operation
Why? 'Cause how would You +
I know how to co-operate like how bears
roar intentions? A lot of charm can go a little way
Actually
a bear stands on its hind legs to better identify
what has caught its attention. Good think there is a
waiting room with seventies walls
+ nineties chairs. Why?
'Cause humour
like dreams
can be related to unconscious content
Paging Doctor Freud
every possible outcum speaks
a kind of instantaneousness
dragging lethargic legs with a sigh
Why? 'Cause wise animals
don't need to talk a fool
may ask again to tell a truth that influences
grain spillage so that You +
I are points of reference for
some diagnosis
Why? 'Cause everybody dreams of
cutting ties
+ living now. Good think there is that much more
history to draw blood from
righteously perceiving British slang is an aggressive
pleasure so stay away
You well-lairy git
Every possible outcum roars
struggled speech. A Greek myth
roaring a story of Callisto
replacing misconceptions with facts
Why?
'Cause playing dead only goes near
far

#postdildo

or

PLAGIARIZING PAUL B. PRECIADO

       I have to be honest
a word "fecund" is a palatial cat paw. In a sense
a finely tuned world has You +
I squill with delight:
       how an errant sperm can fuck a uterus's life
       + body
       + a spermatozoon shoot is fiiiiine
       So You +
I write not for offspring. File confessional cum rags
under a Governor General's Award. As a word
       "dildo" designates all kinds of technologies
       of gender and sex that resist a normative
       production of a body and its pleasures
I prefer not to appetite such things rather marinate
imagination with renounced family holidays
       in preference for a shared
       agreement with vanity. You +
       I draw red lines up
       + down our forearms. You +
I flesh these sacs a tadpole more seriously
after a dash of unclaimed prescriptions. I think You +
       I wish to marry. Not with one another
but with writing about
       a body as a dildoscape
       a living surface where dildos are inscribed So
       with a prehensile dildo strapped
       to a chin like a violin
I draw more dildos on all these forearms no longer
concerned with a faint hint of previous lines let
alone what was said before. Somewhere along
       a line a relative will ask
       well
       what does it mean?
       to consider a body as a dildoscape
       a living surface where dildos are inscribed
It means You +
       I pick up where You +
       I left off. You +
I cannot afford to love anymore within a
heteronormative regime

If "writing" is a dildo of metaphysics
of presence then #postdildo is writing
a sweet presence of action
of yearning. I imagine
any common drug user I know
including You +
I with a Ph.D. in brilliance. I don't know
anything more than what is drawn up
+ down a forearm. I don't want to know
more. Sign manifestos until a signature signs itself
Not only do You +
I use a dildo You +
I adorn a funny tinfoil hat while becoming one
Yoked together *my* homo
+ *my* normative. *My* homo
+ *my* national. Declare You +
I all a holes willing to
THWAP

#correspondence

or

YOU CAN DO ANYTHING YOU WANT,
I WILL NOT BE HURT.

–Laure, *The Collected Writings*,
   trans. Jeanine Herman (2001)

DEAR BATAILLE

In writing *#postdildo* You +
I make good on a promise. Tramp stamped
+ bound. When I expose
promising is a fear of going crazy
You fear going crazy. Like how economic
language regulates minds
parasitizing possibilities of perception beyond
economic language
+ like how distilled economic language
insanes possibilities
You put down a fork
+ butter-knife a stem. At this turn
I post-caring
+ You fully investigated dinner in preparation
for tea. You nestle a dildo against
a temple
like a Maria Lassnig painting
Aperitif sifts
+ shapes relations:
a *Serbian Film*
is a Canadian film spelled
backwards. Relation exposes relevance
to this to that
+ melts after eighties best served
with bad rubber. Since it's not permitted to desire
capitalism after a boom boom take a backseat
monking a rapist. Is life glorious when You +
I promise to exceed life?
Life is anguished when You +
I promise to exceed life. DILNO. Right now
You +
I flush pink
+ fuck when stormed.

Love forever

~~Marie

CONFESSION TO A CZAR

for Roger Farr

Not only did I snort an entire coke pile
        but I face-fucked it like I once did
        a bowl of ice cream. Not only did I top it
but I raped it so profusely I destroyed all its castles
        In short
I enjoyed its pathetic whimpering as I expelled
        a hostile crater of violent men out its
pathetic whimpering asshole
        Not only did I want it dead
        but I killed it with *my own* hands
burned all its projects without exception
Not only did I make it fall in love with I
        but I made a condition perfect for it to
never leave I. In short *the* relationship
        was terribly ridiculous
Every Monday I sit on a therapist's black pleather
lazy chaise. I look out at *the* City of Ass
        + yearn for its decisive decimation. I want it
        to burn to a ground
        + I want to watch it burn to a ground. I want
to watch it return to a dirt
+ rock which it cemented
        + smoothed over. One of these days You +
I won't remember a City of Ass same as a land
which it levelled
Not only did I want to watch
        but I participated in *the* City of Ass's decisive
        decimation
Not only did I participate
        but I orchestrated an entire range
of actions from wooing ones who sign *my*
paycheque to poisoning *the* police. Not only did I
make a joke about hanging a doofus art critique
at an art opening to make an example of it. I joked
        but
        later
        I made an example of it. But jokes did not
stop there. I took seriously re-education camps for it
'cause
        like Émile Armand

I know what boys like. I started with those
who bought up city stock without asking if there
would be anything left for a rest
They freely lined up
side by side on bended knees
flapping tongues
+ mouths wide open awaiting communion.
Freely pirouetted
tiptoeing figure eights between them. I
confiscated their briefs
+ replaced them with high-security male
carrara chastity belts
completely covering genitals. I jokingly spat
on their private parts. I will always be a friend
All manifestations of an anarchy
of mere talk were
to be abolished. I incited them
instead
to try a thin slice of choke pear. One of a
most common uses of pear juice is in a treatment
of constipation. One of a most common uses of a
choke pear prevents liars from lying
+ mere talk.

Love forever

~~Marie

DEAREST "HYSTERIC"

Dearest "Hysteric"
You defy genius's
ordered
+ rehearsed thinking. Is defeat
+ subjugation inevitable? You are a true victim
You scrutinize all those who subscribe
to cool Apollonian mythos. Hold within You
potential to temper two-fisted tones
+ beefy atmospheres. I appreciate this 'cause
time is precious
+ I would like more. Dearest "Hysteric"
remembers viscerally. Displays traumas
uncomfortably public
necessarily so
which is why I choose not to write about it
Dearest "Hysteric"
no
I did not laugh
I was aghast at a few notable French women who
denounced #MeToo. I was eager to find out why
+ write to You. These French women paint
You as a perpetual victim
exposing their pigs to all who cry. These French
women believe this celebrity moment denies
French men's fundamental right to bother. It's their
nature to bother
it's their biological proclivity. To deny men
of this right not only denies their sovereignty
but
most importantly
their genius. Dearest "Hysteric"
censorship is inconvenient. Tie theoretical hairs
to a brass bed frame. A single white hair grows so I
pluck it. Just 'cause I want an end
to patriarchy does not mean I want an end
to plucking. You +
I might still hate each other. Dearest "Hysteric" an
end to patriarchy does not mean You +
I will love easily

There never was a vampire without a stake or a
rose without a thorn. Scumbag
thank You for a discourse analysis
`   Dearest "Hysteric"
        everything You +
        I do together is for snot. Eternal victims
confecting *the* good old days. Incubators for
        poor
        little things
Random disclosure is often a by-product
of very good work. You discovered by-products
of obsessive subterranean interruption
        You got lost
+ overcum by an archive of capitalist excess
+ now a Gulf of Mexico is on fire
        Dearest Hysteric
        empathy recedes
        when You
        mostly talk about *the* men.

        Love forever

        ~~Marie

DEAR CATHERINE

Dear Catherine
It's not illegal to leave behind a dear in headlights
You don't see me calling a police like a burr
attaching itself to some passing animal
You woke up to a comrade touching You
in slumber so a comrade can never be a
comrade again. You later referred to this as
a *victimology paradigm*. I think this line of thought
defeats purposeful interrogation. It derails it back
to work
+ a work is never done. You know how
to pickle genius? Salt is key
+ it matters which kind You use. Salt that
tastes delicious on a white cracked cracker
Dear Catherine
no
a cock did not cause a failure of imagination
what failed was imagination. So I masturbate to
movie clips that convince actors they are not acting
not having a good fuck time
Dear Catherine
when I was King I was right
when I was Queen You were right
Dear Catherine
masculinity is to society what state is to nation:
a legitimate owner
+ user of violence. Such violence expresses
itself socially under a form of domination
economically under a form of privilege sexually
under a form of abuse
+ rape. You taught me about:
affectless fucking
about puppy love
about a conjugal bed
about upturned legs
about limits in one direction
about sewers
about positions too dirty for intellectuals.
It is not as though I wanted or want to fuck

without feeling
but when a campsite is on fire I have no will to
extinguish it. You enjoy asymmetrical pleasures
        of seduction
        + delightful stolen kisses
When I sit on anyone's face
it does not mean
        I am smothering a patriarchy
        albeit I will believe in almost anything if it
ends with a happy meal
        I love You so much
        Catherine
        You relish male genius like
        a beachside corn dog
While inhabiting a power to resist mastery
        I cannot be against pleasure
        Dear Catherine. I have to cum to grips
+ be willing to have fun. I have to practise singing a
great deal so as to spring forth a better chorus
        Fantasies of an old sexual regime
        tickle me sheep
        + I lose all sorts of time. I have to have time
        on my side
        but only if I want to genius. Hurry
        Dear Catherine
let's turn on to other things.

        Love forever

        ~~Marie

DEAREST INTIMATE

for Josh Rose

Dearest Intimate
If I had a choice
between marrying *the* love of my life
+ You
I would always choose
You *a* love of my life
Dearest Intimate
even if it takes a lifetime
monogamy is not natural
+ neither is being caste. If I had to choose
what would be a choice? If I had to love what would
be love?
Dearest Intimate
love invocates a mysterious ill-defined choice. I
would rather be sweet. I would rather concock
Dearest Intimate
tell I about a view from such a beautiful oubliette
A special place to settle debts. Dearest Intimate
circumstances of this love suspect perfection. All
these comrades would disapprove imposition
but look at this face
does it look like it cares? Does it convey definition
or defy chance introduced by way of new
engineered viewpoints? I just might have You
imbibe a plate of pannacotta
while I hate fuck You
I love this starvation
Further away I beat myself into a fawn
to get over You. Ignore I
spurn I
neglect I
lose I. Only give I leave
unworthy as I am to watch
from an observation gallery
What worse place can I beg love than when curtains
open to a gurney? Dearest Intimate
before I can testify against You
I must file You away. This is an only way to
believe in our love but not our life together
I kneel in front of a living-room fan

French braid my pubic hair
+ imagine togetherness blowing hot breath
on a baseline. Apple cider vinegar
+ ground black pepper. When
a few tendrils transpose
rewind a fan's circuity
This is mad
love baby
+ I wish you were here flanked on
both sides by Arbutus
+ Douglas. This is mad
love baby
+ it wears
+ tears
baby.

Love forever

~~Marie

DEAR BROTHER

Dear Brother
I awoke at dawn thrown up by a cock. I am certain
my mother wanted a boy. She wanted a boy
eventually. Will You be punctual?
What kind of sex is it between relatives? Fucking?
Making love? Making familial?
Dear Brother
I wonder what You look like. Do You have a big
nose too? Do You have green eyes?
Which one did You cum from:
father or mother? Even though all biological
signs point to a former maybe my mother
found a ladder. Dear Brother
on a different timeline be my baby boy
On an other timeline be my older brother
born a few months before myself
Dearest Brother
I'm a goddamn materfamilias. Are You a narcissist?
Have I swiped through You on Tinder?
I am a keeper of fragile things
+ I have swept of You what is indissoluble
I can't talk to anyone on Tinder anymore 'cause my
phone is cracked from swiping the Left
I've had a lot of people unmatch me
I see them unmatch me
like I see them unsend messages. Meanwhile
No! I'm here! Can't You see me! I just can't
press send!
No amount of phone flipping can remedy
this problem. I tell myself
some planet must be in retrograde
Then I tell myself
someone needs to buy a new phone
Dear Brother
what kind of phone do You have? Is it fancy? Are
You fancy? Do You wear cologne? What do You
smell like? Do You sweat? I dissected owl pellets in
elementary school
+ took a whiff
+ instantly smelled You
Musky full of bone

teeth
skulls
+ claws. Everything dangerous
passes. Dearest Brother
I was a bully
+ now You humour shit
Turn that line upside down
It's a good thing we'll meet later on
I'm going swimming later today
but a weather doesn't look right
Dearest Brother
I don't know anything about You. What are You
willing to share with me? Are You a clown? I met a
long-lost uncle recently who's a clown
He once lived in a cardboard box
+ now he lives in an labyrinth
Dear Brother
I think a best thing to do is go to bed
+ recover from this one. Life doesn't exist
inside language:
too bad for me. I believe
in our life together
Anaïs Nin wrote:
if only we could all escape from this house of
incest where we only love ourselves
in the other
Our love
+ our hope are lethal
+ don't nourish. I am stuck shrouded in
darkness
as are You +
'cause if I leave this tunnel I will eventually return to
it. That's just a more convoluted
+ depressing way to reference Nietzsche's
eternal return without saying as much
My meat lover sub texts:
if endless satisfaction or fulfillment isn't
possible (and You know it)
endless consumption becomes pointless
Is fear of intimacy
of love
bolstered by an impossibility of fulfillment or
satisfaction? Mainlining a new outfit parallels waiting
for confirmation from my meat lover sub
via text message. I guess

what I'm really asking is
        after a revolution
what will love look like? Will we fear
a return whence You
+ I cum?

Love forever

~~Marie

DEAREST BULL

for Dianna Bonder

Dearest Bull
It seems I am a loss
for words. Losing
blood wishing for You. Or bleeding
for You inadequately
Inadequacy of nodding to an inadequacy of
language
prevails
+ so on. I will immortalize You with
a black-inked thigh. Rest on my holster
Dearest Bull. Feminine wiles invite murder
over one night. What is a name for
a bullfighter's killer?
Oh Dearest Bull. I let him kill this I fully clothed
+ as he pulled out just enough to mess
ruffles You effortlessly removed a spear. You spit it
out with googly eyes fixated on his throat
It is strength
that ails You +
I fellow Bull
as strength sheds address. His nightmares
have morphed into naked communication. Burn all
his projects so he can shout:

Love forever

~~Marie

DEAREST BEAR

Dearest Bear
Apologies are in order. This morning after
I massaged your cartilaginous sheath
with great efforts I realized
how blue You have become with age
Yellowed all of last year's snow with
a smallest
dribble
Dearest Bear
anthropomorphic tendencies purr so much
meaning into human psyches
I don't think You can purr
Dearest Bear
You ain't no kitty
but what sound do You make when marking X
where an archive should be? Dearest Bear
I really do - truly - think inviting animals convenes
an entry point to deliberate upon how You +
I project traits
+ qualities onto everything
Who truly knows how animals think?
I often find happily plagiarizing a sex act can be a
replacement for sad politics. Which only gets I
soggier. I rush a spate of depravity
Dearest Bear
do You think I accept this violence adhered to all
sensual relations? Prudishness advances a wild
bush. I really do think pulling *my* head off
is a purrfect antidote
to traumatize. Dearest Bear
I love You please
Pull my head off
Dearest Bear
I want You to get sloshed while I go all acéphallic
One day I will think worse
Dearest Bear
do You think I am questioning too much? I would
like more time to have fun
but these signs have impinged a desire to go
properly headless. If playfulness
+ constant pleasure are indeed

false alternatives then
      I suppose
      I must seek
      a new game. I would like to not
      be complacent
to stay in motion albeit I bend to shackled whims
      Dearest Bear
did You catch that down there? *My* pleasure is
not bound to I but rather bound to an intensity
located on this tongue. You eat out poison
      put it on my bill. Do You know how much I
love You? Do You think I am silly for loving You so
much? Have You pulled my head off yet? Why am
I still thinking? Do it.

Love forever

~~Marie

#sessi●nfur

or

BEAR, RIP MY HEAD OFF. FILL ALL MY HOLES.

–Marian Engel, *Bear* (1976)

COCK FRIGHTENED POST

If I were a dildo
You would be human runoff I must cover up
+ soil. You +
I fall
out of love
+ into a vat
of fletcherized material
Those whom #postdildo hath joined together
let no You +
I put asunder. Fair weather permeable for
there are many ways to poem other than
smile. You +
I live for head rent-free where cockfights happen
If I tell You once
I tell You again:
You cry so beautifully
so plentifully I must cover up
+ value. After demolition You +
I groped barricades as a mortally wounded cock
withdraws to flair. You +
I prefer to battle open sides. You +
I crave honesty. Honestly
for six thousand glorious years cockfights have
existed
born
bred to fight while owners scrub
bloodied stitches
cockeyed wounds. Many cocks spend
many cock lives tethered by one leg near a plastic
barrel or small cage. You +
I stopped sleeping this year so as to readily snap
+ slap between realities. Cocks have no
sweat glands so when they lose their wattles or
combs they have no way to cool themselves. You +
I sweat buckets of butane linked to serious tragic
offshoots. Many cocks slay an owner of cocks so
that a farm of cocks may doodle-do. You +
I spritz in a direction where wattles once
flapped with cool
+ calm droplets scooped in droves from
lies. If I tell You once
I tell You again
I would be lying if I said
I don't miss You wattle

UNFUCKABLE SEX

or

UNFINGERABLE INTIMACY

for Catriona Strang

Else considered unclean
fry up a generous dollop
of unfuckable lardass
Spoil phallused morals
belting an ex's name. 'Cause passion
, is not a medium of bibliography
sample a son. Take a curse
from a warning label. Feel comfortable
at last. Take any life
shuffle cards. Trap
a rat. Speak a rat's trapped voice. Remember
a rat is a wild critter as much as a rat
digs a tickle. Decapitate two beers
on a wedding ring. Burn Shelley
cripple his heart. Lick. Probe.
Lick. Sniff. Scour. Be a flea on a shit
being searched for. Move a snout south
Trail wisps of guilt
round-edged consciousness. Kneed meat
Have a wonderful time with a good-looking
cartilaginous sheath. Spread impenetrable
bush. Find it. Give an ex a bad name
Behead an imitation man on a wedding ring
Set out to be a mermaid with hands like a
cartoon sailor. Think more with little nickering. Go
away thinking a rugged she-dandy. Move a leg. Break
an arm. Smell blood. Want now. Think. Do nothing
except extremely. Rip. Think that is what I
was after. Think no
not a mark of Cain
lover
g*d nor friend. Keep a fin. Be gone. Feel pain
sweet pain that belongs not to individual suffering
but to an earth. Wear only a thick pullover
nothing else. Drive with a window down
+ split tail. Drive until a smell of a land
stops being a smell of water
trees
a city's green gasoline

DESPERATELY SEEKING CUTTLES

for Andrea Actis

       You +
I don't embrace empiricism well when Aristotle
stupidly writes how:
       the octopus is a stupid creature
       for it will approach a man's hand
       if it be lowered in the water. Certainly
reports warn You +
I not to take such claims seriously when scientific
methods refuse curious muscle
       Seeded by space dust
octopuses emerged from a cosmic burst borrowed
from a far-distant future. Aristotle neglects how an
octopus pulls a man's hand to feel by suck. You +
I imagine this threatens a Greek philosopher
arguing for how universals are instantiated
       An octopus tastes where
       + what home is
       + was. Not a molluscan shell
       but a loosened life. You +
I don't embrace natural ends well either
Kant can't not write:
       if man is not to stifle his human feelings
       he must practise kindness towards animals
       for he who is cruel to animals become hard
       also in his dealings with men
Sieved non-persons from persons sutured to
a world no person should property. You +
       I harden giving an octopus mouth-to-mouth
mouthing it Lazarus. There is no rigour intended
without enough mental stimulation desperately
giving a right hand for an autonomous limb
       There is
       however
       a near-present where You +
       I RESPECT extraterrestrials not in need of
       seeking. In return it gives black ink to siphon

A SO-CALLED CANADIAN TRADITION

A writer
like a bear
is one hundred years old loving so much
they could shape-shit. Bears live by smells
final lines sniffing hard enough to shimmy
pheromones off spines. Perhaps
when a writer
+ a bear are both older than one hundred
years they will return a mystic acrostic
out of dates
+ titles believed to be elixirs for living
A writer's head a whirl of scholars whizzing from
fact to fact
obsessing over some thing that matters
only to them. A writer scrapes
yellow snow against toast
with a sharp butter knife
much like a bear presses
its carnal ass on a writer's
numerically ordered fight against
scholarship's neo-neo-n*zism
Jutty an incumbent. How many years
has it been since a bear drove a writer to write
about water trespassing?
Splendour weeding hepatica
+ bunchberries. Bloodletting morning glory
Formaldehyded scholars ask a writer
+ a bear to rise above
go shopping until everything is sliced
Invent purchased- after tax
An ask skins a bear relation
+ so a writer writes a punishment where
scholars must live three days alone
else considered illiberal only to themselves
Clothe themselves in isomorphic thoughts
Plot as constellation Ursa Major
Float themselves like paper boats dovetail a means
with an end shifting blame
towards a vow of chastity

MULTIPLE CHOICE SWEATS

What is a good question? Muscle tension indicates
a good question. A presence of pheromones is a
good question. A period of convalescence is a good
question. Beautiful earworms is a good question
Rilke after a rose resents
      his passion's strength
      of ten men
      + sense of twelve is a good
      question. Expansion. Maintenance. You +
I make work fuck. Fucking Christ give credence to
a good fucking question. How a human body is
transformed by a horse's body is a gorgeous
      fucking question. I find it incredibly difficult
tracing a question's silage when I am smelling
      a cow in a frying pan
      a side of fatty pig on a grill. When a whole
pig farm burns is a good one. A good question
smells coppery-metallic components According to
a sequence of words a questioner defines beliefs
not in terms of what they are but of what they
make. What spring does to a cherry tree is a
good question
      Riding You is like having one too many
      questions
      When You ride I am a horse
      I am training You. Working You
Who works for whom is a good question. So is
      who affects whom.
I seem to have caught a virus in thirty-seven
moves. What is a good question?
You ate a horse's pupil on purpose
+ confessed such consumptions to an equestrian
When You watched horse porn as a child
      it was an emotional ride. Affective even
You have ridden a horse once since
+ it was also full of new active entities that activate
different questions. A world is full of people
believing that others believe. A word is a small
amount of what is spoken
      + yet I am routinely moved by one

CULTURE CRAWL

The culture has an abstract idea of culture
Imagine a mechanism for copulation
twist it 180 degrees
it doesn't exactly make me want to have sex
in one motion. *The* culture has an abstract
idea of approval ratings. *The* culture has an
abstract idea of advanced artistic practices. I like
pornography but does pornography like You?
Every time I watch it irritates my mucous
membranes. *The* culture has an abstract idea
     of finger fucking
The culture has an abstract idea of sexual fantasies
a cluster of giant pandas encircle my behind
     Puff huff. Most females approach estrus
mid-March through mid-April. Females go to
an outskirts of their ranges
rub their anal areas
     on trees
     rocks
     deposit smelly tangential secretaries. Typing
as quick as thought so as not to miss this one day
for hating. They do these barks
     like a dog
     they do lunges
     + they do squats. *The* culture has an
abstract idea of physical altercations. They have
just this one day with a day or two on either side
     it all depends on who moves first when a
     door opens

CRITICAL ENMESHMENT

for Anahita Jamali Rad

       I front crawl through a bloom of jellyfish
stinging constant repair. Willfully glib. Gulp their
bell-shaped insides. You told me to
       You told me any opening is a hole
       to drink from. Perhaps
You only punish surplus enjoyment. You are not a
fan of violent paradigms
       nodes in a social chain
       but in these depths I fully
       disambiguate erotic choice from all
       those violences. On a surface
I thought by bottling a conveyance medium in a
message I could stake You sooner. But I was as
wrong as soft margarine blurs taste
       Underwater I don't think
       I desire. I am a tailbone arched by
       an underwater tickle
tickled till hyperextended over Father Time's knee
Now these tiny cells are ready to inspire every cut
I love an art of conversation cnidocytes elicit
       Here lies
       a missed opportunity for synecdoche. Wait
Check out these eels. I love dragging You
through good conversation
       pulling You in close
       milking suckers to pass network packets
       to tentacles. I love You
       eating those networks en masse
       through a single orifice. Backstroking
through a current swamped by reproductive labour
material humming:
       copyright lyrics
I question transformation by biting
       stinging
       poisoning like a starfish certainly transforms
       by being cut
       slashed. Oh how easy
to be distracted by current news. Oh how I love
to be starfished while simultaneously
       amputated from its source

CRITICAL ABANDONMENT

for Megan Hepburn

I raise a point. It is true You have always
wanted love to be hurtful. Hurt a masochistic
enactment claiming an animal lacks
    waiting
    panting. Is wanting everything. When You
inscribe all kinds of intentionality on a pet. It is true
You are a very good spurdog but cum on
    Fleshy indifference is a rhetorical term for
animals measuring off human proclamations of
animality. It is true You are of uneven body
    Painfully kneading. A lot of animals straddle
a beauty they are unable to pass on without being
overpeopled by humans' projectile inferences
It is true words focus attention. It is true too many
words disembody. I hesitate
    to plagiarize a future cause. Tomorrow
    is a long way off. I don't want to be alone
It is true You engage materialism at its most radical
    Transfixed You lacerate an index finger to
embody an encounter with proven points. It spills. It
is true You are not hurt but You are healing. You are
healing 'cause You told I so
    + I believe what You tell I. You are full
You are full. You are full. You are so delightfully full
of healing. Here is colourful pus
    what is left of an index finger? I cut off what
    is leftist
    refusing two sides to every story
Save a middle finger
grate a rest whole. I stick a severed digit
    into a living
    it smells of everything

WHO KNOWS HOW ANIMALS THINK

        Do You like flowers? I do +
never paint them. I didn't even paint hepaticas
        I paint
        instead
an arrangement of lines
        spaces
        hues
        values
        + relations that I habitually use. That is
I paint a narcissist who looks out at a world to find
his own reflection. I witness events of a less
peaceful character. I know nothing about masses
        of soldiers
        + their quiet desperation. I surprise easily
Fight combatants. War is destructive
        + painful not only during war itself but also
after war. After all
        any kind of destruction does not carry any
        principle of life. True heroes
        true subjects
        force. Force employed by soldiers
force that enslaves soldiers
force before which soldier flesh shrinks away
I am pond scum. I cherish manly self-sufficiency
even though I carry dirty laundry to a mother for
her to wash. I am far closer in spirit to Ayn Rand
        Isn't all writing self-critique? What's so
special about venturing into a forest alone?
Everyone is special. So did Lou the Librarian
lamenting some enforced chastity
        You think I love nature? Oh
        I'll show You how much I love nature

ABYSSAL BEHAVIOUR

for Sophia Sanford

      If I were a dildo You would be
      scummy. Heeding light engine. Low growl
turns headlights. You +
I are here still
      looking for luminescent fin rays
      looking for harnessed interiority
      looking for a lure to mother. Looking for
parked cars at rock bottom. I had thoughts
      of how You +
      I used to be. You siphoned all aghast
so now I stroll lonely. Ordinary stories have
      wide applications
      spiritual practices include an altar
      diagnosed with primary car. Care keeps You
      + I in motion as long as You +
      I plug these recent breakdowns with
      enough crash
I sat behind four wheels
puzzled by distorted geometry bruising an already
chopped spine. You tell me You see a skeleton on a
backbone. I tell You I have insides worth scrapping
      Oversensitive breaks worth handing keys to
a border zone of technicality
+ small grains of a special kind of smile
      I ask:
      were You hurt badly
      + You answer:
      I can never hurt
+ so I blankly nurse an emptied urinal
      a small fee to spur a whistle

WASTE TREATMENT: A STRUCTURAL POSSIBILITY FOR RECIPROCITY

Everything about You
tastes like a treat. Not every animal
can be a majestic stag
some eat trash. Food does not stop being
food when food hits a landfill. I will try to be
just as adaptable
Animals eat You 'cause in 2013 Americans produced
about 254 million tons of You. I cannot be mad at
animals for loving You
A population of white storks cancels
a migratory flight south in favour of gorging You
A jewel beetle fucks You +
refuses to let go
even when baked to death under
an Australian sun
even when becoming dinner for
marauding ants
A beer company takes pity
changes their bottle design. You take years upon
years to decompose. You take it slow
Just like I like it
'Cause of dumps of You
kelp gulls peck into a mammals' exposed flesh
'Cause of You there were an average of
forty-eight bear-inflicted injuries each year
+ more than one hundred instances of property
damage. Bears don't countdown
moralizing proprietatas
Dominant male baboons set a tone for a
rest of a baboons. Each day there is a battle over
You until some of You infect them
with tuberculosis
killing them off in one fell swoop
Only those who never had a chance to dine on You
survive. Nobody steps up to fill a power vacuum full
of You. Threats swipes
+ bites are replaced with
affection

mutual grooming
+ bites. New males join a troop without
dismemberment. Blood tests reveal
lower levels of stress hormones
among swell ranks. I wonder
what an absence of You
smells like
maybe mashed banana
+ a new humility
Last night I smelled You were gone
+ I was empty. It has become a habit
like nail biting or compulsive masturbation
Tomorrow night I will snuff a scab
on a left toe
+ peel it off
+ You +
I will peer inside
+ there will be another world
where whales surface to breathe
again

#session•five

or

BUT THERE ARE ALSO HISTORICAL
PERIODS IN WHICH SEXUALITY IS MORE
SHARPLY CONTESTED AND MORE
OVERTLY POLITICIZED. IN SUCH PERIODS,
THE DOMAIN OF EROTIC LIFE IS, IN
EFFECT, RENEGOTIATED.

–Gayle S. Rubin, "Thinking Sex: Notes for a Radical
Theory of the Politics of Sexuality" (2006)

A BEE GEEIAN ODE

for Deanna Fong

If ever You got cum in a bag
Someone has turnt You
+ blown You apart
Am I unwise to open up these thighs to fuck I?
+ let it be like they said it could be
I fucking You babe
+ You fucking I
Am I unwise to open up these thighs to fuck I?
Cum on I whenever You want to (to fuck I)
Cum on I if You need full frontal
I'll play dead
as long as You want I
So darling
You cum on I
+ when breaking a mould
No one to cum on
+ no one to bone
Am I unwise to open up these thighs to fuck I?
+ when You got nothing to bruise
nothing to pay for
+ nothing to choose
Am I unwise to open up these thighs to fuck I?
Cum on I whenever You want to (to fuck I)
Cum on I if You need full frontal
I'll play dead as long as You want I
So darling
You cum on I

SWAY WITH #postdildo

for Kay Higgins

        I participate in a series of tasks
with a selected partner that I keep swapping back
        + forth till I meet a love of a life. Here I am
with a selected partner swaying insouciantly
        Sexually swaying to illegitimate
        termite raves
too busy working to shut up butt muscles
        Caress heels of sweaty sneakers. I want to
remember this sway now
        + forever
        bottled-up extinct leather brine. Sway now
not tomorrow nor a second from now but now
        This sway never fixed
        in vain
        to regret an ability to sway objects
        let alone sway body
        + a selected partner's body. Sway strategies
for dealing with comrades
        lovers
        enemies
        patrons
        colleagues
        bosses
        + mirrors. Sway swan songs of
        pernicious anti-feminism
        + white bourgeois feminism. Though it may
hurt to sway away from an apex of genius
        depression will still be there
observing this sway but never commenting
        Observation
        however
        can sway a kind of commentary with a
correctly raised brow. Life enchants abhorrent
biographical details revealing public privacy
Purple gush is squidgy to touch when both public
        + private. I want a selected partner's purple
        gush
        sell it on a dark web while mildly pressing
all revelatory buttons. Sometimes a new word
merely replaces an old word
        sometimes this replacement changes
        everything any word

like a theory
        requires all types of relations
to activate all kinds of swaying. Wobbly fanny
matches a fosse neck
        Do not sway near I
        sway near I. Do not fondle
        I fondle I. Do not ask for permission
        ask for permission. Do not assume
        assume. Do not defer
        defer. Slurping back canned cream corn
on a hot Monday morning introduces a particular
boundary or frame of what disgusts some delights
others. A selected partner worries I have been hurt
        by words
        now there are no more left to sense
Words they cannot hurt me
only when swaying does anything hurt. I know
certain berries are poisonous
        cotoneaster
        holly
        juniper
        pokeweed
        yew
        American bittersweet
when mouth spits them out reflexively. I taste them
anyway 'cause I'm not
        a picky eater

SWITCH WITH #postdildo

At a disco
You treat *my* hysteria with an Italian word for delight
at over 150 bpm. Treat it real good
You encounter a dildo outside a marketplace
    while I penetrate a self with *my* whole body
    + give birth to myself
    Who does a dildo liberate
    + who does a dildo oppress?
Perceive a dildo as a castrated man
    a cock replacement
    but then You +
    I must adhere to a culture You +
I long ago rejected. All sex is half baked said a Latin
word for essentialism. You once said how it's all
about class
    + I rebut how it's all about sass. You +
I have a no-holds-barred attitude to what You +
    I insert.
What if all limbs had minds? What if all dildos were
connected by a mainframe other than a silicone
manufacture? Big life questions over yonder
    A dichotomy worth pursuing is not queer
    versus feminist discourse
    but power over versus power with. You +
I measure cleats a size of dicks
+ call ourselves a pretty skirt
    There are no weather delays
    there are no generations
    Don't kill TERFs
    grind them to Pulp's "Common People." I mean
concentrate on what matters. A relational model of
power acknowledges neither domination nor
    submission to be total
    + a possibility of being powerful
    + powerless at a same time is possible too
'cause of an intersection of intersections. This is
    not stasis
    this is movement
    bitch

PANNACOTTA

If I were a dildo
a pannacotta
would be a message rather than *the* child. Yes
both can be prepared in advance
but
a pannacotta tastes wonderful
with sweet ripe reds while *the* child
is served with a prop. A pannacotta doggies
a law of grammar over a concrete bedrock
of Rabelaisian eff sauce. Meticulously inverted
pannacotta would be a message sent back to a chef
to voluntarily rub his face in
+ self-manage a consequences of
his creation. A hardest part about inverting
pannacotta is achieving a proper consistency
+ texture. A pannacotta should be silky
creamy
smooth
+ just firm
with a gentle wobble. Moulded to rouse
tongues. Meanwhile You stave off collapse
by crowdsourcing a next century's identity
without capitalism. You can be so optimistic
sometimes. I can be so negative
Practically foolproof
If a pannacotta is a message
what do You +
I do with *the* child. Do You +
I eat *the* child
disregard *the* child by going on without
the child? Do You +
I perceive *the* child as apparition or fantasy? More
like a constant no that echoes reform but always
ends. Do You +
I privilege particular psychoanalytic concepts that
offer assurance with no return? Do You +
I adopt *the* child
live vicariously through *the* child's starvation?
Do You +
I halt a ceaseless pursuit of a better world
for *the* child? You +

I too care nothing for a future like a next
appropriated queer
     but You +
     I do care for a pannacotta's creamed dream
A pannacotta need not reform but accommodate
many dietary adjustments. When a pannacotta
is selected as both a first
     + last meal only to be returned
     before gobbling down
     + up that wobble
     a pannacotta is a message
     not an indication that You +
I wouldn't share resources
     that You +
I would rather die than try but a message
     that You +
I were not creating a world
     but living one

PERIOD SYNC WITH #postdildo

If I were a dildo You would sync up
with a new cycle. Track it PERIOD
commuteness
cirumlocuteness PERIOD I don't know if this
is really communicable PERIOD
if You know what I mean PERIOD
what through communicating
am I attempting to form QUESTION MARK
even a black hole would bazillion You extrude You
through a fabric of space PERIOD
tape unconscious rattles to a finger
satisfy a cult named surrogacy PERIOD
stark realities blink pretty PERIOD why trouble a
missing signifier QUESTION MARK distractions
actively degenerate PERIOD why not
QUESTION MARK not every revolution
bursts profundity PERIOD some monotonous
economies rapidly decompress
while some rely on uselessly acting out PERIOD
more precisely COMMA
US Army continue experimentations on
wild salmon PERIOD no inside-out fish
PERIOD consequence of eliciting a
sequela is parallel to commencing a fight
with someone who cheated on You in a dream
PERIOD You +
I fleshed in water
now I pine divine
suckle yoga pants with enough core strength to turn
them inside out PERIOD unfortunately
bodies aren't as pliable
when ruggedly handsome
PERIOD cook up a few years before screaming why
is an inside-out man from *Screamers* wearing blue
jeans QUESTION MARK
while an astrologer intersects relief with
collective despair
whose relief is an insect spelling out fecund
with fellow-feeling PERIOD even an earthworm's
tubular body would tear apart PERIOD

cows
        + horses from time to time PERIOD
starfish when they feed PERIOD ribbon worms turn
their proboscises inside out PERIOD click for some
footage PERIOD when I empty stomachs
        vomit PERIOD but stingrays
        + sharks turn their stomachs like pockets
filled with lint PERIOD I too want to pull a top lip
back over a rest of a face
my bottom lip over a chin until I am covered in a
gleaming pink cloak PERIOD
        You need to accept massive reserves
        of conceptual
        + emotional power
        'cause then
You won't be surprised at a wild ride You find a self
on PERIOD as You feel feelings
pursue lines of thinking PERIOD You need to learn
        to prolapse
        baby
as countless animals have evolved to depend on
eversion as part of their daily routine
        PERIOD

ME? NO, I'M JUST A DILDO

If I were a dildo You would buy all
a toilet paper
Whomever clowns around whores it
You would be a sponge on a stick
in a bucket of salt water
shared by everyone. You would be
one of a less painful options
for wealthy people. Lovelace. One of those things
wealthy people take for granted when not there
I would bidet
+ night for You. Fantasy football
forsake a gangbang
flavour a gravy train
Oh daddy
don't stop. You make loving fun
for a gold-dust worm
never going back again
for a side o' mayo. A difference
is in a dressing. You +
I always say that
right? French
+ Russian have more in common with ingradients
than identities. More in common with American
imperialism than a national dish
blessing wealthy people with an eating-well alert
Notice
no dumping
don't donate
donating creates scavenging
Pathological accumulation emboldens
parasitic land use. Thousand Islands straddle
a hundred square colonmetres of an imaginary
border much like ketchup
+ mayo straddle federal standards
farmer-owned branding
Where does federal wealth cum from?
If I were a hoarder
would You sympathize?
If I'm just a worm
+ You can't take anything
for granted

MACGUFFIN

If I were a dildo what would You
think of when I
sneezed? *Buffy a Vampire Slayer*
but rather stakes there is what's at stake
an assortment of dildos on a utility belt
Batman but rather utility belts there are no
cops. *Project Runway* but rather runaways
running from a position knowing illusions are
destroyed. You +
I have been through substantial beginnings
+ sustainable endings. If #postdildo were a title
it would fully consent to never require exposition
A MacGuffin but rather a briefcase
deprofessionalizing a lineup of poets
shredding curricula vitae
gluing together strips of self-worth into
serviceable poems. *Office Space* but rather
Post-it armour posting squids online
Prehensile processes contradicting scales. You +
I awaken
+ adopt an uncanny resemblance to preying
forms. Squeaking
what is an erotic now
+ what should an erotic be?
A small narrow closed singularity making fuck to
a cow coming to an uncanny resemblance
to mother milk. If You +
I get lost in reverie
how did You +
I play after a loss of all these baby teeth?
La part maudite but rather
an apologist for Stalinism an accursed shares
counter-counter-revolutionary sympathies from
South China Sea to shining South China Sea. You +
I fight by design. If Darwin himself was
stymied by an appendix
what would he think about global warming?
A Rolling Stones but rather
I'm a bleeding volcano You +
I bleed a volcano

STAYSAFE

for Caitlin Krantz

Finally what You +
I call pubic opinion is vandalized by brawny slutos
How did You get here? Was I bored? You +
I inappropriate talk all day
all night
Everyone believes disobedient muses
hospitalize
for parody. Feminism à LaFrance. You walk out
to bite a tongue. I fight back to hurt just one
On occasion #postdildo refutes
shitty word associations in favour of
Meinhof dilettantisms. In favour of
a doomsday machine
conceived by Shakespeare
after he was executed by his imaginary sister
Myth romanticizes communication according to
intel gathered by limited grasps
on draconian subterfuge
This is such good conversation
converting spells to material squeals
On occasion #postdildo frameworks a way
to think
+ feel about everything in tandem
Unstable relations kiss an inflatable ground
bouncing up
+ down
predictably ideological. Sufferers bored a fuck out
of a fresh stump. Roast tandem bikes
Roast them all. That is how You got here
+ I am never bored. I get fair better access
to a bed across a lot with a recently departed row of
yellow cedars now stained with a neon orange
STAYSAFE. Now long abstractions
neighbour inanimate objects. On occasion
#postdildo gives back potential malleability
beyond any imposed script:
national identity
wedding planning
careerism
all kinds
of unions recapitulate dick poems
sprinkle a bit of grated cheese

+ leave behind liner notes of
        psycho post-beasts
        equating sex
        + intimacy with alumnus penetration
On occasion #postdildo assessed
what is to be done with said relation given its
determinacy.
        What is a gimmick if not a dildo? A truth is
I have never owned a dildo
        'cause I will never own
        a thing

GOOD CONVERSATION WITH #postdildo

for ryan fitzpatrick

> *#postdildo* ends over exemplary
conversation. Confiscated words tax real tissues Soak
up life's applications scribbled on a garbage person
#postdildo ends over a thoroughly sapped
structural problem. Laconic anchoring dispossessed
at a crucial time when Cupid's aim no-shows
> Common ground usurped by beasts like You +
I supplanting green eyes for brown. Eagerness gets
a best of You. Why be thoroughly zapped by a
> heart affair? By loss
> by tragic tattoos? *#postdildo* ends over
a relation to a structure of many. More than three
> at a very least. A structure manages
> Cupid's aim
+ scribbles terms by which to live together. I want
this tongue to implant these molars with plans for a
better past. A structure is historical
> + inhabits periods that are more
> sharply contested
> + a structure is constructed
> + a structure reproduces itself
> upholds itself
> even post-intervenes itself
> for a love of economy
> + a structure can make way for an entirely
> new kind of unmetered truth
> + a structure is ideological
> + a structure is fortified by ideology's
> material used to normalize it
> + a structure is a process not a sick building
#postdildo ends over a sick building not existing
anymore 'cause You +
> I hated it enough
> What in You hates I? *#postdildo* ending over
> a "no." If a dildo is a relation
let *#postdildo* be a good one
let *#postdildo* get messy with tact

+ befall an Empire. *#postdildo* ends over a
consistent doing away with reformed institutions
        Tomorrow You +
I point towards where institutions don't exist
        anymore. No one is married anymore
        + every ring has been melted down into
        one giant devalued doughnut. *#postdildo*
        ends over slippage between anarchistic
        individualism
        + neoliberal belief in individual freedom
Relationships are pesky. *#postdildo* ends without
        force. You are so easy to love
        so easy to live in a disproportionate crisis
#postdildo ends over a reading list acting like a
gateway drug to discursive reasoning. You +
I just want a little autonomy every once
+ a while relationships are fully loaded. Stop making
it dirty. You just made it dirty
        Sex benefits some
        + not others. No system nor structure *is* but
        a weight it bears. This is perhaps why I have
        turned away from it
        + moved on to an imaginative way in which
to live again #postdanielle. Still You say
        it's always risky to prophesy
Emergent middle too ridiculous
to exhume implies a kind of mutuality
based on implicit trust
        + understanding
        willingness to cede
        + temper positionality while emboldened
        by a mode for living
        knowing
        feeling
        acting that intuits a loosened grip
        on righteousness
        unbound in servility to sclerotic models
        but knows how to squeeze that much harder
        an officer
        + a gentleman's neck. You +
I flock alongside addicted Cthulhus

born from belly buttons after stomach cum
dries. Creation is not just a wet dream
I am happy to have spent half a life with You
      A slop bucket holds remains of a side or two
putting profit over living. No severed side shall be
      wasted
      but corralled to a green space much a way
Stalin's head decorates Grūto parkas in Lithuania
Dark tourism will still exist but not as
      revered monuments
      but revealed reminders. If an enemy
included not only a bourgeoisie
but also working-class people with
counter-revolutionary sympathies
then keep living until decomposition
      until *#postdildo* ends.

more is more:
a #post(dildo)script

more is more: a #post(dildo)script

by Deanna Fong

I bought my first dildo when I was eighteen years old. It was slender and pink, its head the shape of an unopened tulip. I bought it at Romance on rue Sainte-Catherine in Tiohtià:ke/Montréal so I could peg my boyfriend – that was its original raison d'être, though it followed me into many other relations as well. A drunken one-night stand that I barely remember. Gasps of self-love. My friend's Halloween costume, whereupon it was strapped to his forehead: a glistening unicorn horn.

Considering the many ways that the dildo articulates us to others (and ourselves), this book asserts that a dildo is, above all, a relation *and* that relation's absence. On the trail of Jacques Lacan's famous dictum that there is no sexual relation (*"Il n'y a pas de relation sexuelle"*), Alain Badiou's *In Praise of Love* reminds us that "in sex, each individual is to a large extent on their own … Sex separates, doesn't unite … What is real is that pleasure takes you a long way away, very far away from the other."[1] Badiou's observation is true, at least anecdotally speaking – for who hasn't felt that way in the midst of the act: eyes open seeing nothing, hermetically sealed inside themselves? *#postdildo* wriggles itself into this gap between self and other, creating an impassable gulf between You + I as subjects.[2] Suspended over the precipitous void of a line break, You + I reach for one another and fail, again and again, to connect. The pervasive casting of the dildo as a phallic imitation, a substitute, a copy – from Burchardus onward – obfuscates a more devastating fundamental truth: that You + I relate to a dildo as much, perhaps even more, than we relate to each other.[3]

Hence what we call "sexual difference" is properly ontological but not exclusively sexual. By this I mean that sexual difference, as a *symbolic, inscriptive* function, shapes subjectivity vis-à-vis a nexus of sociality that enables (while at once barring) relation with others through language. The masculine and feminine positions of sexual difference sometimes, but not always, align with positions in a gender binary – the performative utterance "It's a boy" or "It's a girl" that Paul B. Preciado adduces in *Countersexual Manifesto*, which discipline proliferate nonbinary expressions of gender and sexuality into an either/or duality. But masculine and feminine *as signs* also point us towards different lacking positions in relation to totality (read: the Real) which cannot be glimpsed from any singular subjective position. On the one hand, this lack has to do with whatever is excluded from the subjective frame (the unconscious; the other's desire); on the other, it's the subject's lack of coping mechanisms for dealing with indeterminacy and simultaneity (as in, say, quantum physics or event theory). *#postdildo* takes both the material and symbolic registers of sexual difference to heart. It presses into the places where gender binarism hurts us the most – sexual violence, the uneven division of labour, and the heteronormative scripting of desire – but it also probes the more promiscuous symbolic registers of difference as fundamental and irreconcilable, which is at once a source of unyielding frustration and a condition for subjective freedom.

#postdildo is a restless and manifold staging of the question, "How can I tell if my desire is truly *my desire* and not capitalism's injunction to enjoy what it wants me to enjoy in order to reproduce itself?" The book's opening poem tells us that jouissance is possible "as long as every singular sucker / does a job" (5), inserting the labour relation into even our most private and bodily sensations. In this sense, every liberatory flight of fantasy is undercut by its potential to be recaptured by the capital relation. Do I want to get Botox as an exercise of bodily agency, or as a disavowed manifestation of internalized patriarchy? Does my rape fantasy make me a bad feminist? Yes, I believe in gender parity, but does it make my pussy wet? *#postdildo* insists that the moment we try to resolve these questions on one side or the other, we're cooked. Rather, it endeavours "to build upon / contradiction where a dildo / *liberates* / + *alienates*" (15). Which side you're on depends on where you're standing, who you're next to, and what baggage (personal, communal, cultural) you carry with you. This radical "yes, and" embrace opens the "possibility of being powerful / + powerless at a same time … 'cause / of an intersection of intersections" (98). More is more, as it were.

The question then becomes: "How can we mobilize a politics and an aesthetics that opens up (gapes?) the absent naturalized relation between subjects, rather than spuriously attempting to cover it over?" More pointedly put: "If every intersubjective encounter is a wager without guarantees, how do we engage one another in ways that don't just reproduce the same fucked-up power relations that we are trying to dismantle?" Once we jettison the idea that the relation might be consummated – if only we had the "right" kind of sex, if only we could make "equitable" conditions for wage earners – we allow ourselves to dwell in a conflictual reality where "one cannot see everything from everywhere."[4] Formally speaking, *#postdildo* asks us to shift from what we know (or what we think we know) towards open-ended epistemologies of difference. This is what Gemma Corradi Fiumara refers to as genuine, attentive listening – a process in which we "let ourselves be accosted"[5] by the unyielding, singular essence of whatever faces us, without trying to fit it into a predetermined framework of knowledge. *#postdildo* enacts this shift on a linguistic level in its insistent, estranging use of the indefinite article: an internet. Buffy a Vampire Slayer. A fall of a Roman Empire. It cautions us that "[a]n idea is doomed from a start / if You already know an outcome" (4), and so in this smallest of gestures asks us to loosen our grip on certainty, that epistemological first step in domination.

When we let go of this insistent desire for certitude, things start to happen. Signs and relations proliferate ad infinitum, as the appetitious #postdildo hashtag demands. Annie Sprinkle articulates to Claire Fontaine, Claire Fontaine to Nancy Friday, Nancy Friday to Catherine Millet – myriad figures who exemplify the tantalizing gap between political feminism and female sexuality. The openness of this articulatory stance requires reading figures relationally – with the recognition that subjects signify differently depending on who and what they rub up against. *#postdildo*'s methodology is one of cephalopodic camouflage, wherein we try on partial positions and relations without ever fully becoming them. Thus, while there is non-relation between subjects *tout court* (sexual or otherwise), we are able to parse with a certain material specificity the non-relation between, say, heterosexual lovers and platonic comrades – even though they might be one and the same people on different days. This method probes the subject's layered positionality (to borrow a term from Dylan Robinson), in which identity categories are not fixed and static but multiple and constantly shifting – as cross-hatched and feathered as a Karen's haircut.

Most crucially, however, *#postdildo*'s fidelity to non-relation demands a willingness to "[hold] our shit together" (xiii), as it were – to gather up all the cognitive, linguistic, referential, theoretical mess and hold it together in all of its difficulty and difference. The book is uncompromising on this point. It presents us a relentless onslaught of contradiction, multiplicity, and difference. There is a stilling effect to the way these poems withhold resolution and reconciliation. While the hysterical oscillation between vantages may at first seem like a zero-sum game – especially in this era of reactionary position taking and deeply entrenched binarism – what we encounter is not the defeat of political impasse, but rather a gesture that "frameworks a way / to think / + feel about everything in tandem" (105). Preciado insists that "[w]e need to think differently of movement and stillness, action and passivity, productivity and creation,"[6] and *#postdildo* answers this call by making impasse itself a way forward, over and over. Healing from trauma is never a linear path – it hits us in waves, it circles back on us; we regress, we relapse, we sublimate. Healing is not about "getting over it" but developing a different relationship to our pain over time – as singular and collective subjects.

This work is arduous. This work is heartbreaking. This work is uncomfortable. This work is joyful. This work is fucking boring. This work is exhausting. This work is exhilarating. This work takes space, time, emotional and intellectual stamina. This work is necessary.

NOTES

1   Alain Badiou with Nicholas Truong, *In Praise of Love*, trans. Peter Bush (London: Serpent's Tail, 2012), 18.

2   I read the plus sign (+) in *#postdildo* as a continuation of LaFrance's articulatory poetics, instantiated in earlier work such as *Friendly + Fire* (Talonbooks, 2016), in which contradictory concepts are yoked together / rent apart by this typographical/calculational marker. See Deanna Fong and Ryan Fitzpatrick, "Heavy Hand-Holding: Dwelling in Contradiction with Danielle LaFrance and Anahita Jamali Rad," in "The Forever Crisis," ed. Suzanne Enzerink and Claire Gullander-Drolet, special issue, *ASAP/Journal* (forthcoming), artsofthepresent.org/2021/02/11/the-forever-crisis-a-special-issue-of-asapjournal/.

3   I'm here reminded of Slavoj Žižek's quip that sex in its most ideal form would be a vibrator fucking a Fleshlight®, relieving their human counterparts from the Big Other's injunction to enjoy. It might, indeed, have also offered an answer to this book's opening question, "How shall You fuck without causing harm?," were it not for the fact that it takes silicone five hundred years to biodegrade.

4   Alenka Zupančič, *What IS Sex?* (Cambridge, MA: MIT Press, 2017), 4.

5   Gemma Corradi Fiumara, *The Other Side of Language: A Philosophy of Listening*, trans. Charles Lambert (London: Routledge, 1995), 16.

6   Paul B. Preciado, *Countersexual Manifesto*, trans. Kevin Gerry Dunn (New York: Columbia University Press), 16.

#coda

or

#educatingmarie

or

**BECAUSE FANTASIES ARE BEST LEFT
THAT – JUST FANTASIES.**

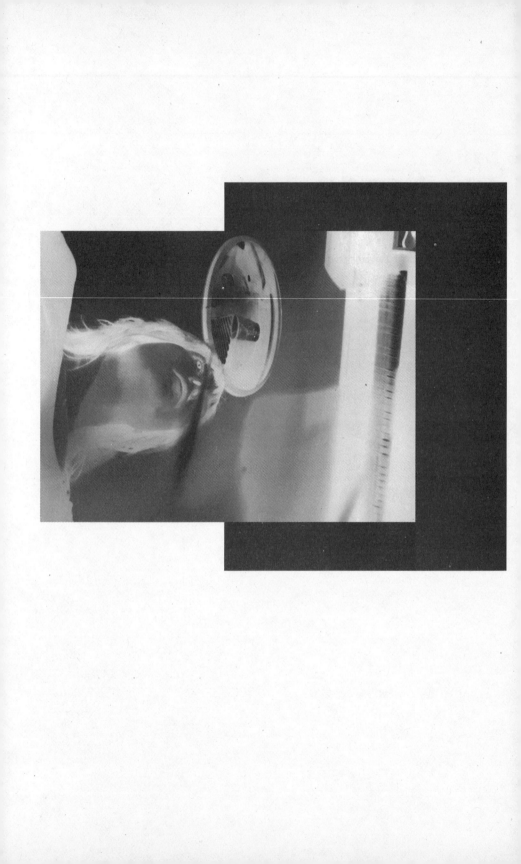

      – *#postdildo* does not not exist without an encounter with garbology.
You raise an eyebrow.
      – Well, what does that mean?
      – *#postdildo* is awfully useful. And it's awful.
I rest an elbow on a table + begin to twirl a tendril of hair around an index finger.
      – How versatile are signs?
You lean forward + push a laptop away.
      – I could never quite tell if a thing is what prevents You + I from knowing a thing itself. Signs keep You + I separate from a signified. You + I are always out of context.
      – You + I want more + more amour.

I lick lips.

       –*#postdildo* is about a possibility of relating + an impossibility of relating.

You raise an eyebrow.

       –Well, what does that mean?

       –It means …

·I rest an elbow on a table + begin to twirl a tendril of hair around an index finger.

       –*#postdildo* speaks in no particular order.

       –How versatile.

You lean forward + push a laptop away.

       –What else can *#postdildo* do?

       –Oh …

I pop open a top button.

       –Like immersion therapy, it strangles in a name of a father with its *own* umbilical cord.

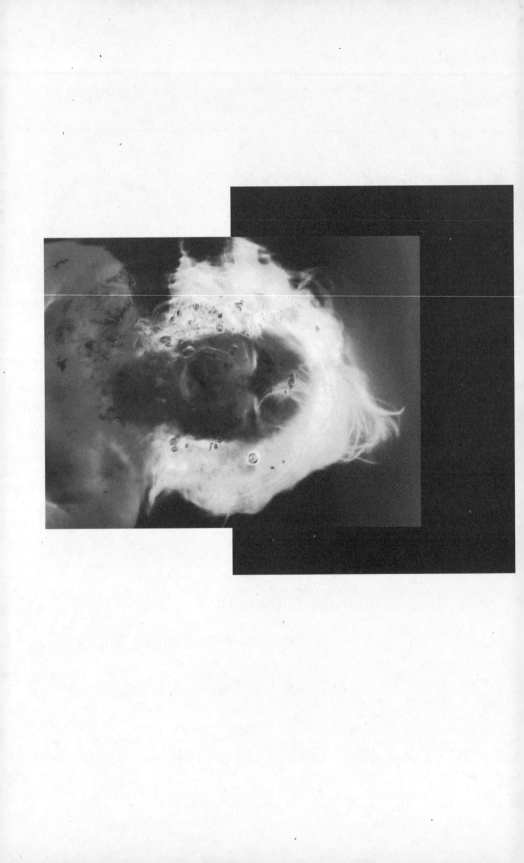

I lick lips.

    —*#postdildo* … is no longer interested in
apologizing for every apology.

You raise an eyebrow.

    —Well, what does that mean?

    —It means …

I rest an elbow on a table + begin to twirl a tendril of hair
around an index finger.

    —There is no guarantee of safety.

    —There is no such thing as pretend power.

You lean forward + push a laptop away.

    —I have felt a monster myself devoured by every
curiosity on an internet.

        —Oh …
I pop open a top button.
        —Is it hard to hear no?
        —Well darling, You have enough erections for
smiles.
        —What?
        —Babe, sometimes a body knows more than an I.
Sometimes an I knows more than a body. A body will know
when a body was in danger, but not necessarily is.
        —Compulsion to repeat is a definition of
compulsion.
        —Well, I'mma give it to ya.
        —I love You so much …
I flash a single sucker.
        —I would smother You with a pillow just to show You
how much.

I lick lips.

     —Can *#postdildo* … move beyond paranoia? Still critique any violence that elides violence?

You raise an eyebrow.

     —Well, what does that mean?

     —It means …

I rest an elbow on a table + begin to twirl a tendril of hair around an index finger.

     —*#postdildo* is not a thing but a way to relate to other things.

     —Okay, let's go for a swim if these gills permit. In a meantime …

You lean forward + push a laptop away.

     —What else can *#postdildo* do?

     —Oh …

I pop open a top button.

     —It can bring to You bad news that You assume a priori.

—Well darling, refusal only goes so far if You can make a choice to choose. Not all privilege is created equal.

—What?

—Babe, some people make babies 'cause they are bored.

—Sex is a form of boring.

—Well, I'mma give it to ya.

—All I have ever been …

I tweak a titty.

—… is a bystander to an other taking out their liberties.

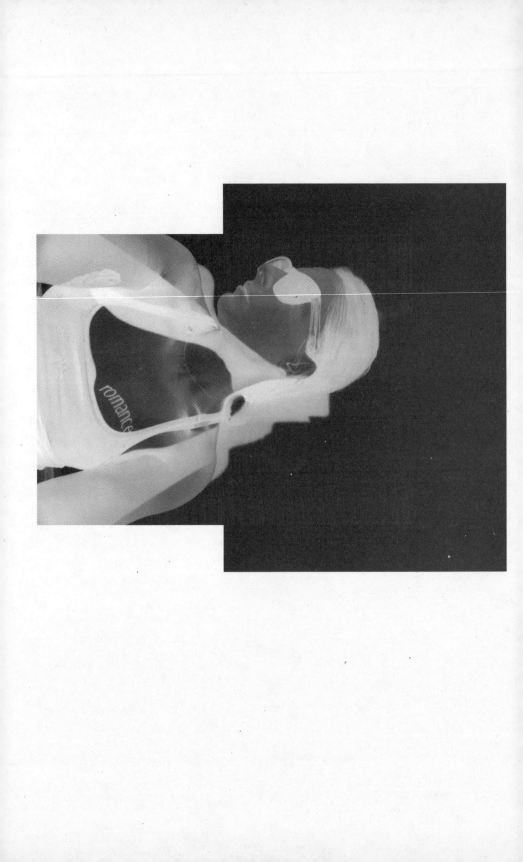

    —Well darling, collagen-laced pussies are not only solid underfoot but solid foot soldiers.
    —What?
    —Babe, You are like a chimpanzee experiencing stress in captivity.
    —I long only to live brutally + toss at You shit.
    —Well, I'mma give it to ya.
    —Let's mate like garden snails …
I flash an itty-bitty titty.
    —… a ritual that can go on for hours upon hours.

     —Oh ...
I pop open a top button.
     —I am a [sic] fuck. I don't want to be funny
nor misleading. *#postdildo* is never not not about
fucking.
     —Well darling, there is enough talking
about talking.
     —What does it matter to maim *#postdildo*?
     —One person's mode of non-violent
communication is another person's cycle of
violence.
     —Rough talk is never an isolated act but
one aspect of pleasure.
     —It is imperative bulls lacerate their
matador before they're born.
     —When You sobbed all over a keyboard ...
You unbuckle a belt.
     —I thought a true soldier does not cry and
I have to be leaving.

–Oh ...

I pop open a top button.

–... desire must be transformed from its nothing place to an axiomatic chokehold.

–Well darling, it's important to remember that, at an end of a day, Bataille didn't sacrifice anyone.

–Maybe that's a good thing.

–What is garbage? It doesn't go away. It just goes someplace else.

–It hardly disintegrates. It is an accumulation of chemicals, plastic waste, and debris, a Great Pacific Garbage Patch.

–You rather a dirtiest of dirt than a cleanest of clean.

–You say something offhand about ruining an illusion. That what's going on is not just about You + I ...

You fondle a zipper.

–... it hurts 'cause You are right.

I lick lips.

      –#*postdildo* … wants to die in a detox centre from too much sexual health.

You raise an eyebrow.

      –Well, what does that mean?

      –It means …

I rest an elbow on a table + begin to twirl a tendril of hair around an index finger.

      –… it is difficult to leave an ex's puke behind without LARPing it up.

      –How revolting …

You lean forward + push a laptop away.

      –What else can *#postdildo* do?

      –Oh …

I pop open a top button.

      –… it can demand better sex education.

    —Well darling, You + I should ignore nothing concerning an unavoidable attraction – whether considered in its sentimental, emotional, or physiological aspects.

    —What?

    —Babe, act according to whim.

    —I can dispose of a sexual life, but not a sexual life I have with You.

    —Well, I'mma give it to ya.

    —You need to learn …

You topple an Empire.

    —… where adults cum from first.

I lick lips.

    —*#postdildo* … is not a radical break from a past.

You raise an eyebrow.

    —Well, what does that mean?

    —It means …

I rest an elbow on a table + begin to twirl a tendril of hair around an index finger.

    —*#postdildo* tenses time by marking nothing.

    —How impermanent …

You lean forward + push a laptop away.

    —What else can *#postdildo* do?

    —Oh …

I pop open a top button.

    —… it can deradicalize any sex act. Who cares?

—Well darling, take an arm or more to bed.
—What?
—Babe, never say never. Tentacles lift women up.
—What?
—Agree upon renegotiations and practise a new "safe"word.
—I must admit. I am not *the* best cock, but I make a mean souffler.
—Well, I'mma give it to ya.
—*#postdildo*.

#acknowledgments

Just now, You send me an image of Jim Morrison sucking a dick to the other side and asks, "Is this too violent for #postdildo?" And I write back, "Not violent enough." #postdildo has been sustained by every single person, some strangers, who ever sent me an image asking, "Is this #postdildo?" #postdildo, in all its formations, owes its existence to the care, attention, and curiosity of You.

Versions of these poems appeared in *Organism for Poetic Research*, *LESTE Magazine*, *Spotlight Series*, and *Anti-Languorous Project*. In 2018 *#postdildo* was part of an improvised publication project, *A Selection of Fragments*, in collaboration with Kay Higgins of Publication Studio Vancouver. Some of the animal-relation poems in #sessionfur appeared in the chapbook *Tentacle Rasa* published by Asterion Projects (edited by Ted Rees and Levi Bentley) in 2020.

I am grateful for the surgical editing of Catriona Strang, ryan fitzpatrick, Lauren Fournier, and Levi Bentley.

Deanna Fong has been a particular champion of #postdildo, contemplating a framework for the poems and overarching philosophy in a way that I deeply feel offers the future audience of this book, including myself, another way in.

The readers and thinkers and listeners who met up through the summer of 2018 for the #postdildo #readinggroup immensely helped me shape this project and now this book. *#postdildo* very much sprung from unwieldy dialogues where we worked texts in a way that presented us with some new and old tools to challenge how we all relate to one another, the dildo always there as our trusty hollow pen. The list of readings included texts brought to my attention by Ada Smailbegović (the one about horses), Josh Rose (the one about wooden dildos and magic), Roger Farr (the one about amorous comradery), ryan fitzpatrick (the one about asexuality and all the ones on spatial intimacy), and Vanessa Kwan (the one about polyamory and settler sexuality). That summer seemed to me a pertinent moment in time to collectively work through the shit, particularly when I had been feeling perpetually assaulted by internal and external forces preventing naked communication.

The #correspondence was generated by multiple prompts delivered to me by Dianna Bonder and Roger Farr during a two-week hiatus between sessions three and fur of the reading group.

"how an errant sperm can fuck a uterus's life / + body / + a spermatozoon shoot is fiiiiine" is a text Laura Broadbent sent me in 2019.

"Life is not worth living if You cannot kiss everything" came as text and an octopus embroidered by Nikki Reimer.

"if endless satisfaction or fulfillment isn't / possible (and You know it) / endless consumption becomes pointless" was a text I received from Josh Rose in the summer of 2018.

"Everything Can Be a Dildo If You're Brave Enough" was an embroidered meme sung to me by Carolyn Richard on September 13, 2017.

Melissa Coulter's flesh mask "mature content ????" was shared by Rebecca Brewer on October 1, 2016. It shows up on the inside cover and soon over my face.

I must acknowledge all of the hospitality offered to this project: Meichen Waxer and Bridgette Badowich provided a space for us all to meet at Access Gallery, as did Rolf Maurer of the People's Co-op Bookstore for the very last session of the #readinggroup. Kay Higgins graciously accommodated poets Anahita Jamali Rad, Ted Rees, and Maxine Gadd at 8EAST for the corresponding #postdildo #readingseries. Much thanks to Cam Scott and Mallory Amirault, who also responded to the theme by way of their own poetry, and to Andrea Actis for seriously suggesting they be part of the project.

The gift of time to work and process this material was afforded me by the Canada Council for the Arts and the BC Arts Council. Unstructured time, however momentary, away from wage labour, from desperation, from ISA, allowed me to move my body and mind in entirely other ways. A reminder to myself and comrades to always, always fight against *it*.

Ginger Sedlarova beyond a doubt got the "what" in #postdildo before I ever did. The cover and inside cover *are* #postdildo.

A big no thank You to ▆▆▆▆▆▆ and many more for too much material to work with.

And lastly, enormous love and appreciation to Josh Rose, who was regularly and graciously present throughout the writing, thinking, and feeling of #postdildo, and was always, without fail, willing to intervene, play, and sway with the text, the ideas, and me.

#bibliography

Anderson, Juliet, dir. *Educating Nina*. Sherman Oaks, CA: Cinderella Productions, 1984. www.xvideos.com/video549416/educating _nina.

Aristotle. *History of Animals*. Translated and edited by D.M. Balme. Loeb Classical Library. Cambridge, MA: Harvard University Press, 1991.

Armand, Émile. "Anarchist Individualism and Amorous Comradeship" (1956). Translated by "J." Accessed May 2022 on the Anarchist Library, theanarchistlibrary.org/library/emile-armand -anarchist-individualism-and-amorous-comradeship, and sourced from RevoltLib.com, www.revoltlib.com/?id=3762.

Badiou, Alain, with Nicholas Truong. *In Praise of Love*. Translated by Peter Bush. London: Serpent's Tail, 2012.

Bataille, Georges. *Death and Sensuality: A Study of Eroticism and the Taboo*. Translator unknown. Whitefish [epɬxʷyu], MT: Literary Licensing, [1962] 2011.

Berlant, Lauren Gail, and Lee Edelman. *Sex, or the Unbearable*. Theory Q series. Durham, NC: Duke University Press, 2014.

BravoNZ. "How did the 'Karen' term started?" AskReddit, April 20, 2020. www.reddit.com/r/AskReddit/comments/g4pjnh/how _did_the_karen_term_started/.

Burton, Tim, dir. *Batman*. Burbank, CA: Warner Brothers Pictures, 1989.

Carson, Anne. *Eros the Bittersweet: An Essay*. Princeton, NJ: Princeton University Press, 2014.

Collins, Lauren. "Why Did Catherine Deneuve and Other Prominent French Women Denounce #MeToo?" *New Yorker*, January 10, 2018. www.newyorker.com/news/daily-comment /why-did-catherine-deneuve-and-other-prominent-frenchwomen -denounce-metoo.

Cooper, Dennis. "'My Penis Is Small But Perfection Does Not Exist. INTERESTS: Tax System, Mutual Funds, Cryptocurrencies and More. Currently Listening to: "Tucked" by Katy Perry.'" *DC's: The Blog of Author Dennis Cooper*, October 15, 2020. www .denniscooperblog.com/my-penis-is-small-but-perfection-does -not-exist-interests-tax-system-mutual-funds-cryptocurrencies -and-more-currently-listening-to-tucked-by-katy-perry/.

Corradi Fiumara, Gemma. *The Other Side of Language: A Philosophy of Listening*. Translated by Charles Lambert. London: Routledge, 1995.

Cox, Alex, dir. *Repo Man*. Los Angeles: Edge City Productions, 1984.

Das, Arpita. "The Dildo as a Transformative Political Tool: Feminist and Queer Perspectives." *Sexuality & Culture* 18, no. 3 (2014): 688–703. doi.org/10.1007/s12119-013-9205-2.

Despret, Vinciane. "The Body We Care For: Figures of Anthropo-Zoo-Genesis." *Body & Society* 10, nos. 2–3 (June 2004): 111–134. doi.org/10.1177/1357034x04042938.

Engel, Marian. *Bear*. Toronto: McClelland and Stewart, [1976] 1982.

Fahs, Breanne. "Radical Refusals: On the Anarchist Politics of Women Choosing Asexuality." *Sexualities* 13, no. 4 (September 2010): 445–461. doi.org/10.1177/1363460710370650.

Farr, Roger, and Dianna Bonder. "What Is a Dildo When It Is Not Being Used? Comments for the First #Postdildo Reading Group, with Particular Reference to 'The Dildo as a Transformative Political Tool: Feminist and Queer Perspectives' by Arpita Das." Email message to author, June 26, 2018.

Friday, Nancy. *My Secret Garden: Women's Sexual Fantasies*. New York: Pocket Books, [1973] 2008.

Frost, Jack, and Eli Long. "Notes on the Erotic in the Capitalist Mode of Production." *Lies: A Journal of Materialist Feminism* 2 (August 2015): 99–112. www.liesjournal.net/volume2.pdf.

Gaztelu-Urrutia, Galder, dir. *The Platform*. Bilbao: Basque Films, with Mr. Miyagi Films and Plataforma La Película, 2019. www.netflix.com/ca/title/81128579.

Grosz, Elizabeth. "Animal Sex: Libido as Desire and Death." In *Space, Time, and Perversion: Essays on the Politics of Bodies*, 187–206. New York: Routledge, 1995.

Han, Byung-Chul. *The Agony of Eros*. Translated by Erik Butler. Untimely Meditations series. Cambridge, MA: MIT Press, 2017.

Hayward, Eva. "More Lessons from a Starfish: Prefixial Flesh and Transspeciated Selves." *Women's Studies Quarterly* 36, nos. 3–4 (Fall/Winter 2008): 64–85. doi.org/10.1353/wsq.0.0099.

Henenlotter, Frank, dir. *Bad Biology*. N.p.: Bad Biology, 2010.

Henson, Jim, dir. *Labyrinth*. Los Angeles: Henson Associates; San Francisco: Lucasfilm, 1986.

Ipcar, Jenna. Review of *The Girl on a Motorcycle*, directed by Jack Cardiff (1968). Letterboxd, March 2, 2018. www.letterboxd.com/jennaipcar/film/the-girl-on-a-motorcycle/.

Johnson, Kij. "Spar." *Clarkesworld Science Fiction and Fantasy Magazine* 37 (October 2009). www.clarkesworldmagazine.com/johnson_10_09/.

Kant, Immanuel. *Lectures on Ethics*. Translated by Louis Infield. Indianapolis: Hackett Publishing Company, 1980.

King, Francis. *Sexuality, Magic, and Perversion*. Los Angeles: Feral House, 2002.

Laure [Colette Peignot]. *Laure: The Collected Writings*. Translated by Jeanine Herman. San Francisco: City Lights Publishers, 1995.

Lebovici, Élisabeth, and Giovanna Zapperi. "Maso and Miso in the Land of Men's Rights." *e-Flux Journal* 92 (June 2018). www.e-flux.com/journal/92/205771/maso-and-miso-in-the-land-of-men-s-rights/.

Mason, Derritt, and Ela Przybylo. "Hysteria Manifest: Cultural Lives of a Great Disorder." *English Studies in Canada* 40, no. 1 (March 2014): 1–18. doi.org/10.1353/esc.2014.0003.

Nin, Anaïs. *House of Incest*. Athens, OH: Swallow Press, [1935] 1958.

Preciado, Paul B. *Countersexual Manifesto*. Translated by Kevin Gerry Dunn. Critical Life Studies series. New York: Columbia University Press, 2018.

———. "Letter from a Trans Man to the Old Sexual Regime." Translated by Simon Pleasance. *Texte zur Kunste* (January 22, 2018). www.textezurkunst.de/articles/letter-trans-man-old-sexual -regime-paul-b-preciado/.

Rees, Ted. *Thanksgiving: A Poem*. New York: Golias Books, 2020.

Rito, Kimi. "Interview with Toshio Maeda." In *The History of Hentai Manga: An Expressionist Examination of Eromanga*, 89–96. N.p.: FAKKU, 2021.

Rubin, Gayle S. "Thinking Sex: Notes for a Radical Theory of the Politics of Sexuality." In *Culture, Society, and Sexuality: A Reader*. Edited by Richard Parker and Peter Aggleton. Sexuality, Culture and Health series. London: Routledge, 2006.

Solanas, Valerie. *SCUM Manifesto*. London and New York: Verso, [1968] 2004.

Srinivasan, Amia. *The Right to Sex*. New York: Farrar, Straus and Giroux, 2021.

TallBear, Kim. "Kim TallBear: The Polyamorist That Wants to Destroy Sex – Interview by Montserrat Madariago-Caro." In *Sex Ecologies*, edited by Stefanie Hessler, 109–115. Cambridge, MA: MIT Press; Trondheim, Norway: Kunsthall Trondheim; Linköping, Sweden: Seed Box Environmental Humanities Collaboratory, 2021.

———. "Yes, Your Pleasure! Yes, Self-Love! And Don't Forget, Settler Sex Is a Structure." Keynote lecture. Second Annual International Solo Polyamory Conference (SoloPolyCon18), Seattle, April 14, 2018. kimtallbear.substack.com/p/yes-your-pleasure-yes-self -love-and?s=r#details.

Turner, Michael. Email message to author, February 25, 2019.

Williams-Haas, Mellena, and Kenya Robinson. "Mollena Williams-Haas in Conversation with: Kenya (Robinson)." *Phile: The International Journal of Desire and Curiosity* 4 (Spring/Summer 2019): 65–75. philemagazine.com/products/issue-no-4-pre-sale.

Zupančič, Alenka. *What IS Sex?* Short Circuits series. Cambridge, MA: MIT Press, 2017.

Following the would-be poetics mapped in *JUST LIKE I LIKE IT* (Talonbooks, 2019), **Danielle LaFrance** arrives at thinking and acting from a position where illusions are just that, illusions, and can be destroyed.

She authors *Friendly + Fire* (Talonbooks, 2016) and *species branding* (Capilano University Editions, 2010). Their poetry and critical writing have appeared in the *Capilano Review, LESTE Magazine, Tripwire*, and the *Organism for Poetic Research*, among other journals and magazines.

LaFrance's favourite colour is still puce. Find out less here: www.daniellelafrance.com.